MORE SONGS OF THE SIXTIES
THE DECADE SERIES

CONTENTS

ABRAHAM, MARTIN AND JOHN

Words and Music by
RICHARD HOLLER

5

ALFIE
(Theme From The Paramount Picture "ALFIE")

Words by HAL DAVID
Music by BURT BACHARACH

Very Slowly, Rubato

10

ALL MY LOVING

Brightly, with a swing feel

Words and Music by JOHN LENNON
and PAUL McCARTNEY

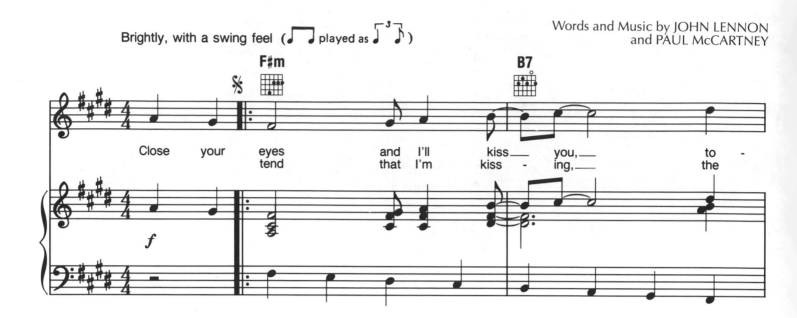

Close your eyes and I'll kiss you, to -
tend that I'm kiss - ing,

mor - row I'll miss you; Re - mem - ber I'll
lips I am miss - ing And hope that my

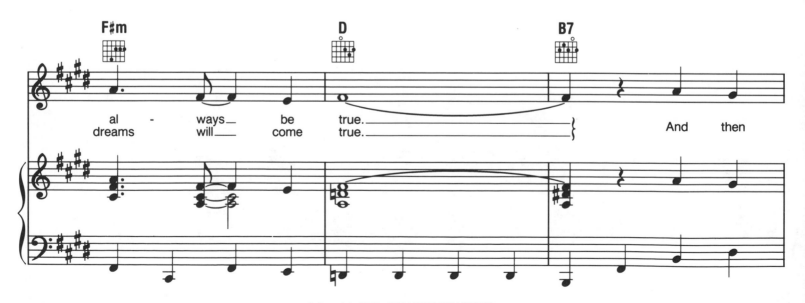

al - ways be true.
dreams will come true. And then

MCA music publishing

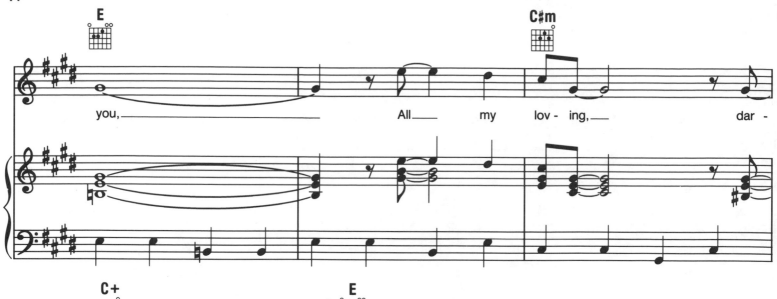

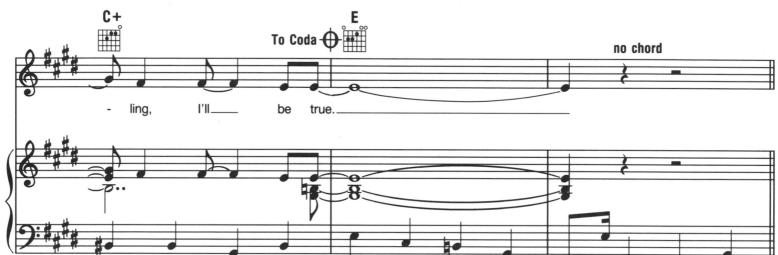

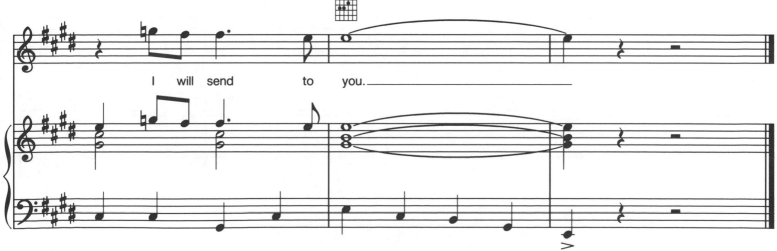

ARE YOU LONESOME TONIGHT?

Words and Music by ROY TURK
and LOU HANDMAN

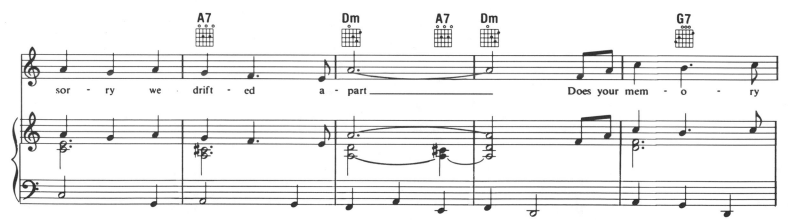

AND I LOVE HER
(From "A HARD DAY'S NIGHT")

Words and Music by JOHN LENNON
and PAUL McCARTNEY

BABY, IT'S YOU

Words and Music by MACK DAVID,
BURT BACHARACH and BARNEY WILLIAMS

Moderately

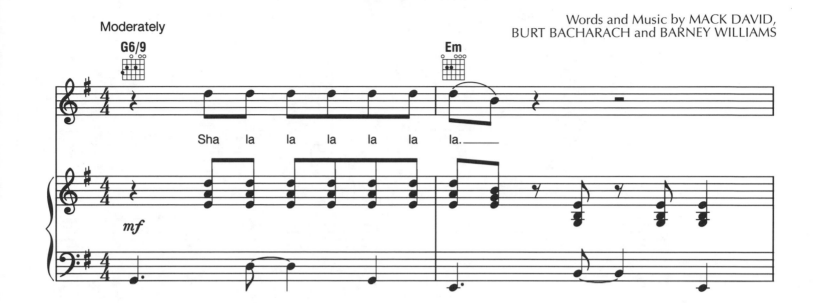

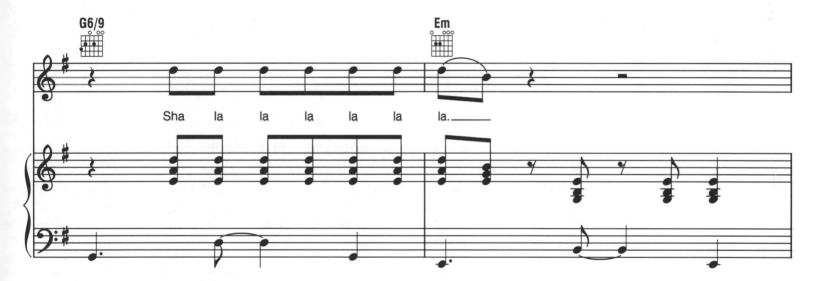

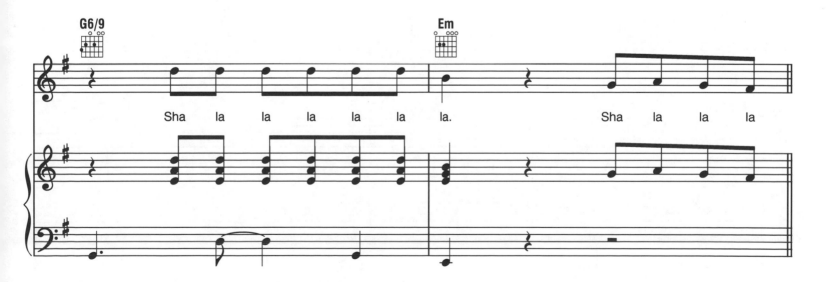

BABY ELEPHANT WALK

(From The Paramount Picture "HATARI!")

By HENRY MANCINI

Moderately slow and steady

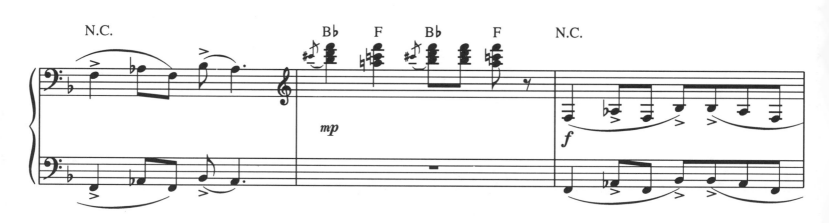

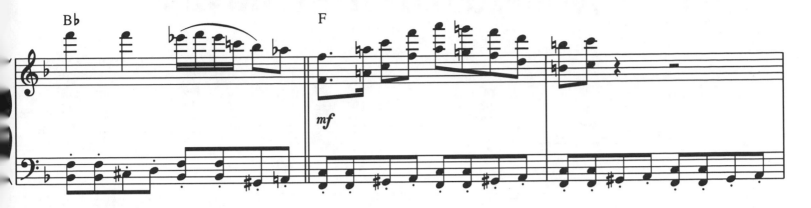

(IT'S A) BEAUTIFUL MORNING

Words and Music by FELIX CAVALIERE
and EDWARD BRIGATI, JR.

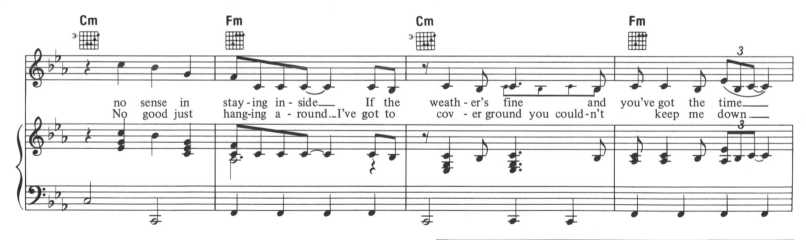

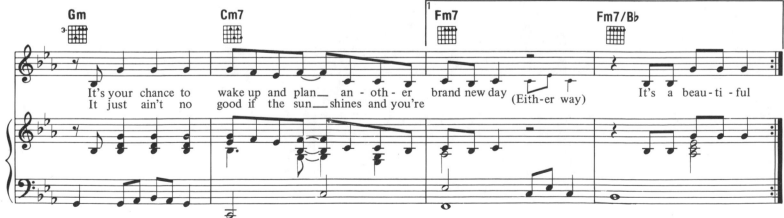

BEYOND THE SEA

English lyric by JACK LAWRENCE
Music and French lyric by CHARLES TRENET

Slowly

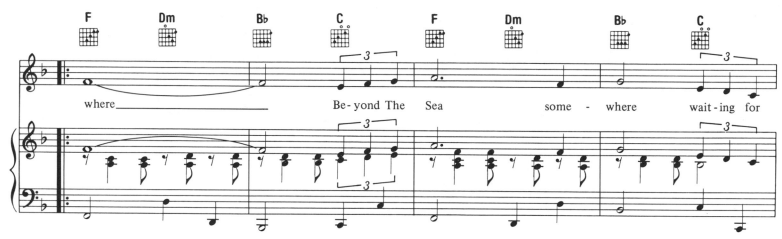

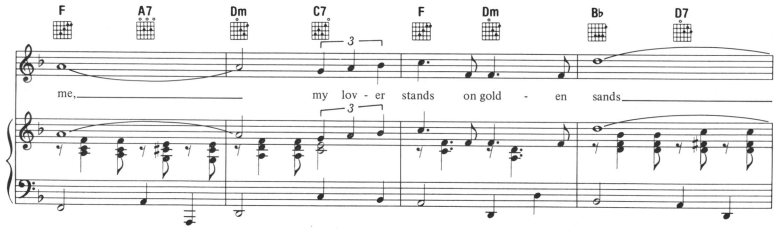

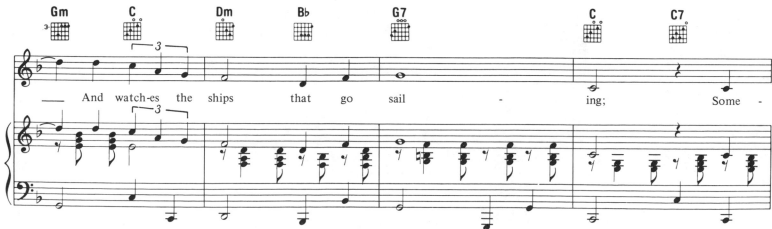

BONANZA
(Theme From The TV Series)

Words and Music by RAY EVANS
and JAY LIVINGSTON

MCA music publishing

BLUE VELVET

Words and Music by BERNIE WAYNE
and LEE MORRIS

Slowly with expression

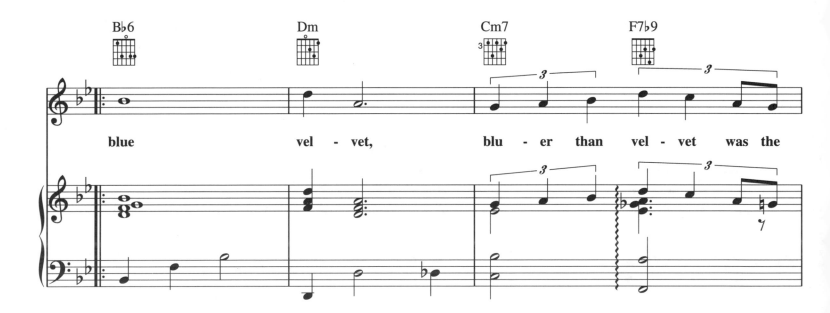

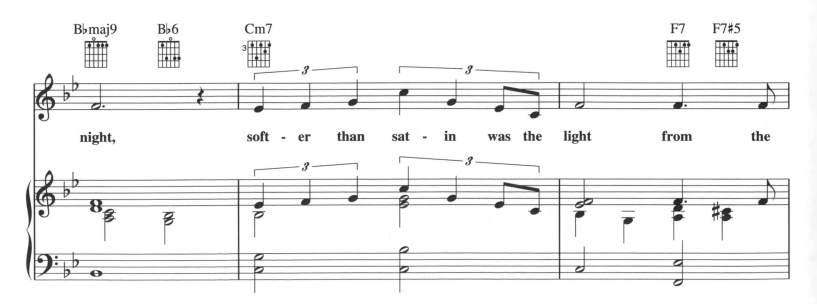

BORN TO BE WILD

Moderate Rock

Words and Music by
MARS BONFIRE

1.,3. Get your mo-tor run-ning._ Head out on the high-way_
2. I like smoke and light-ning,_ heav-y met-al thun-der_

look-ing for ad-ven-ture in what-
rac-ing in the wind_ and the

ev-er comes our way._ Yeah, dar-ling, gon-na
feel-ing that I'm un-der._

MCA music publishing

COME SATURDAY MORNING
a.k.a. SATURDAY MORNING
(From The Paramount Picture "THE STERILE CUCKOO")

Words by DORY PREVIN
Music by FRED KARLIN

Moderato but not too slow

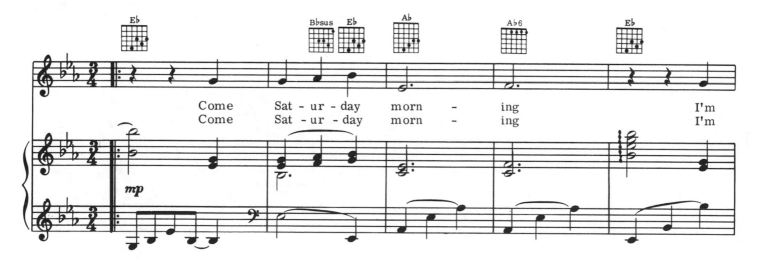

Come Sat-ur-day morn - ing I'm
Come Sat-ur-day morn - ing I'm

go - ing a - way with my friend; We'll
go - ing a - way with my friend; We'll

Sat - ur - day spend till the end of the day.
Sat - ur - day laugh more than half of the day.

Just I and my friend.
Just I and my friend.

We'll trav - el for miles in our Sat - ur - day smiles,
dressed up in our rings and our Sat - ur - day things,

and then we'll move on.

But we will re - mem - ber long af - ter

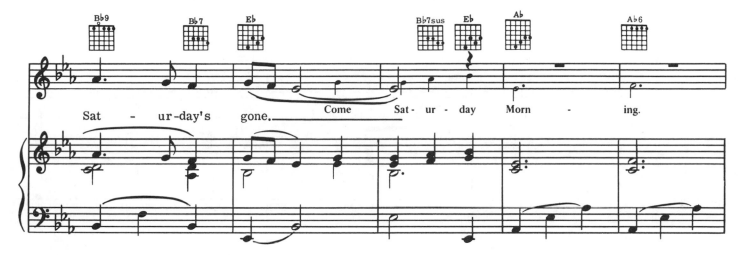

Sat - ur-day's gone. _____ Come Sat - ur - day Morn - ing.

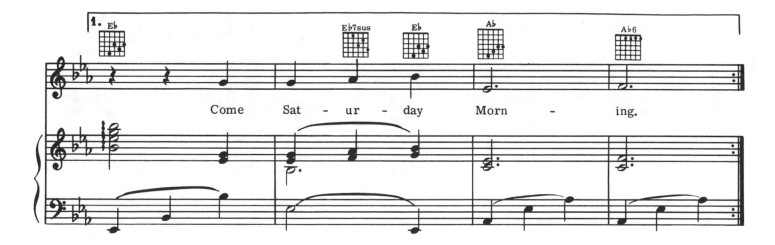

1.
Come Sat - ur - day Morn - ing.

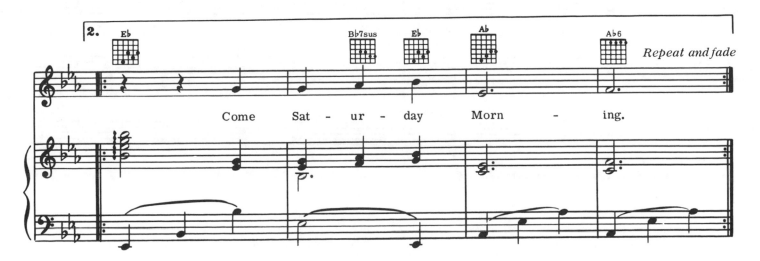

2.
Repeat and fade

Come Sat - ur - day Morn - ing.

CALL ME

Words and Music by
TONY HATCH

*Chord names and diagrams for guitar.

MCA music publishing

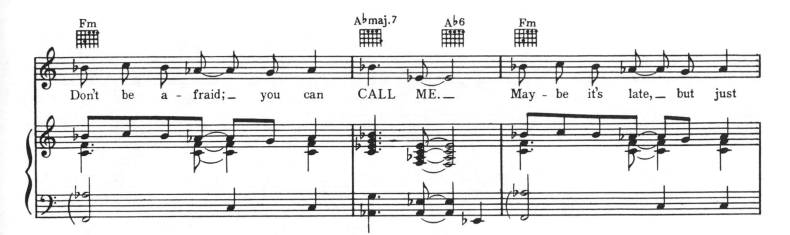

Don't be a-fraid;— you can CALL ME.— May-be it's late,— but just

CALL ME.— Tell me and I'll— be a-round.————

When it seems your friends de-sert— you, there's some-bo-dy think-

-ing of— you. I'm the one who'll nev - er hurt— you.

CALL ME IRRESPONSIBLE
(From The Paramount Picture "PAPA'S DELICATE CONDITION")

Words by SAMMY CAHN
Music by JAMES VAN HEUSEN

CAN'T BUY ME LOVE

(From "A HARD DAY'S NIGHT")

Words and Music by JOHN LENNON
and PAUL McCARTNEY

Can't buy me love, _____ oh, _____ love _____ oh, _____ can't buy me love, _____ oh. _____ I'll

buy you a dia-mond ring, ___ my friend, ___ if it makes you feel al-right, ___
give you ___ all I've got ___ to give ___ if you say you love me too, ___

Instrumental Solo

CHERRY, CHERRY

Words and Music by
NEIL DIAMOND

Ba - by loves me, yes, yes, she does.
Y'ain't got no right, no, no, you don't,

Ah, the girl's out - a - sight, yeah.
ah, to be so ex - cit - ing.

Says she loves me, yes, yes, she does.
Won't need bright lights, no, no, we won't.

61

To Coda ⊕

Tell your ma - ma, girl, ___ I can't stay long.
No, we won't ___ tell a soul ___ where we gone to.

We got things ___ we got ___ to catch
Girl, we do ___ what - ev - er we

up on. Ah, you know,___
want to. Ah, I love ___

CRAZY

Words and Music by
WILLIE NELSON

Moderately Slow

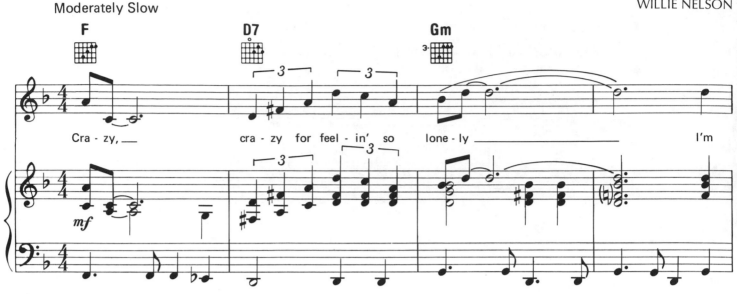

Cra - zy, __ cra - zy for feel - in' so lone - ly _____ I'm

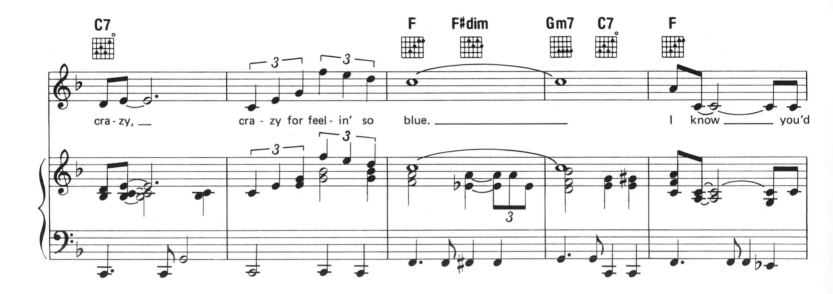

cra - zy, __ cra - zy for feel - in' so blue. _____ I know ____ you'd

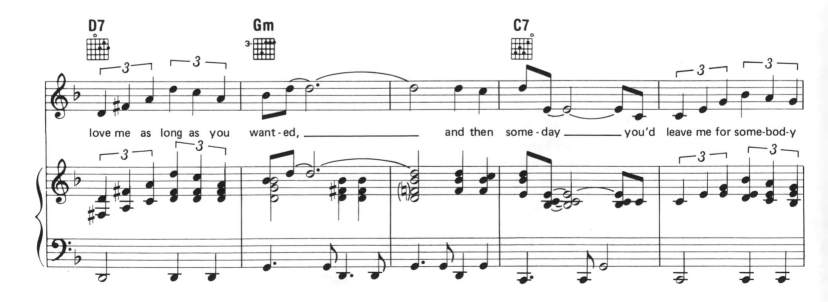

love me as long as you want - ed, _____ and then some - day ____ you'd leave me for some - bod - y

new. _____ Wor-ry _____ why do I let my-self wor-ry, _____

_____ won - drin'___ what in the world did I do? _____

Cra - zy _____ for think - ing that my love could hold you, _____ I'm

cra - zy for try - in', cra - zy for cry - in' and I'm cra - zy for lov - in' you!

DON'T LET THE SUN CATCH YOU CRYING

Words and Music by GERARD MARSDEN, FRED MARSDEN,
LES CHADWICK and LES MAGUIRE

DON'T SLEEP IN THE SUBWAY

Words and Music by TONY HATCH
and JACKIE TRENT

Medium beat

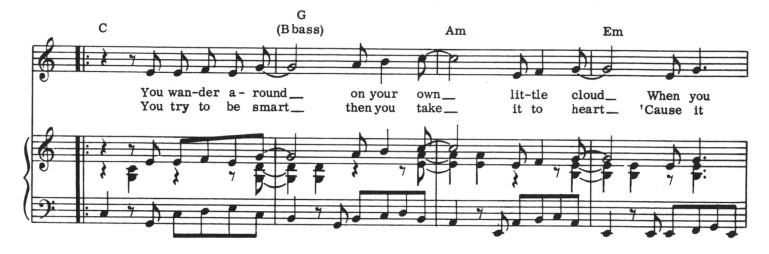

You wan-der a-round__ on your own__ lit-tle cloud__ When you
You try to be smart__ then you take__ it to heart__ 'Cause it

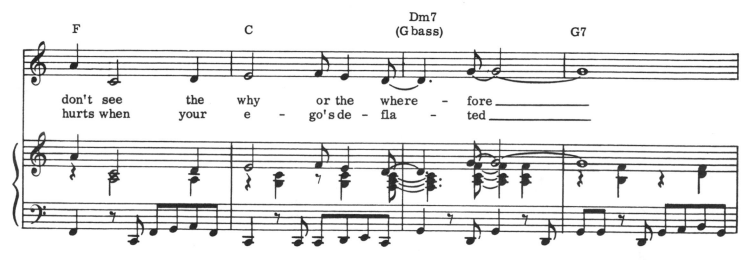

don't see the why or the where - fore _____
hurts when your e - go's de - fla - ted _____

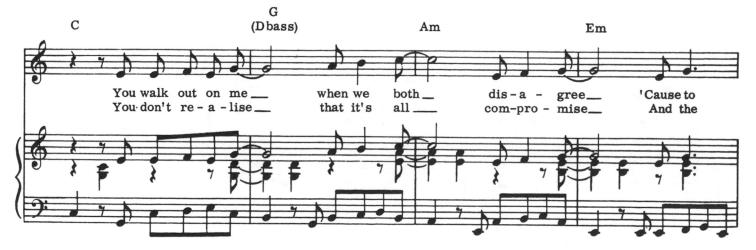

You walk out on me __ when we both __ dis-a - gree__ 'Cause to
You don't re-a-lise __ that it's all __ com-pro - mise__ And the

MCA music publishing

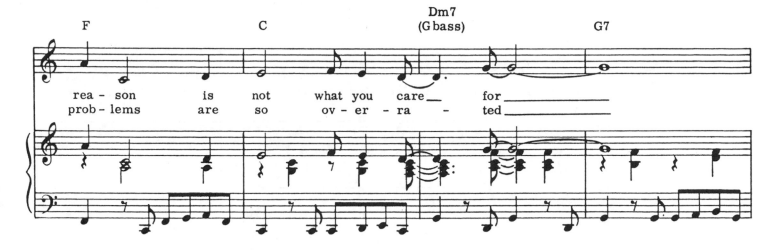

reason is not what you care___ for _____
problems are so ov-er-ra-ted _____

I've heard it all a mil-lion times be-fore
Good-bye means noth-ing when it's all for show

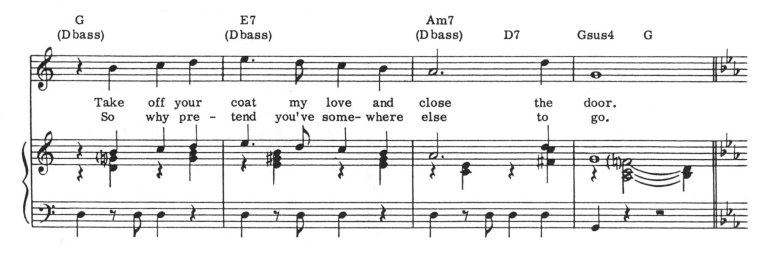

Take off your coat my love and close the door.
So why pre-tend you've some-where else to go.

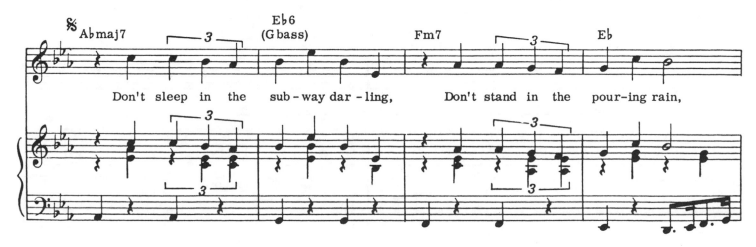

Don't sleep in the sub-way dar-ling, Don't stand in the pour-ing rain,

72

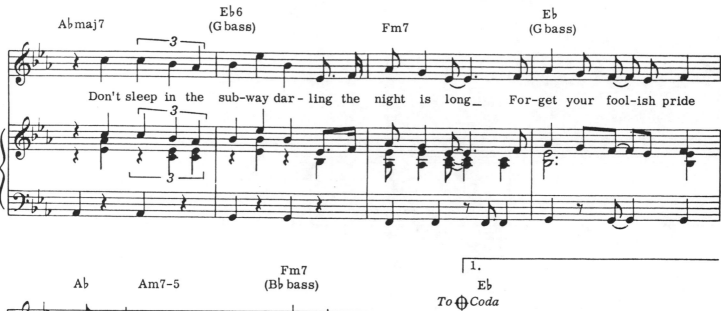

Don't sleep in the sub-way dar-ling the night is long_ For-get your fool-ish pride

noth - ing's wrong_ now you're be - side_ me a - gain.

gain.

gain.

EARLY IN THE MORNING

Words and Music by MIKE LEANDER
and EDDIE SEAGO

Medium Bounce

VERSE

Eve - ning _____ is the time of day _____
Night time _____ is - n't clear to me _____

I find _____ no - thing much to say } _____
I find _____ no - thing near to me } _____

don't know _____ what to do _____ but I come

MCA music publishing

ELEANOR RIGBY

Words and Music by JOHN LENNON
and PAUL McCARTNEY

Moderately, with a steady beat

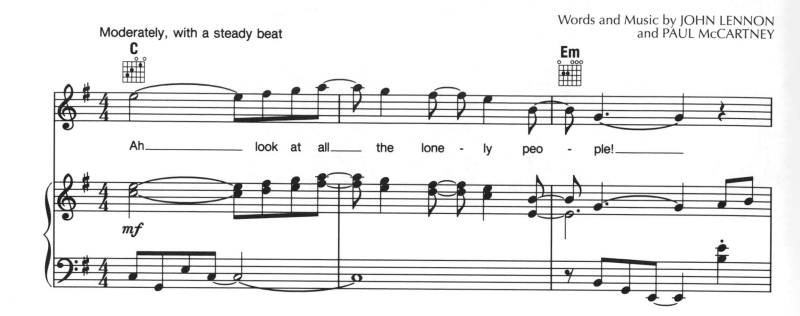

Ah_____ look at all___ the lone - ly peo - ple!_____

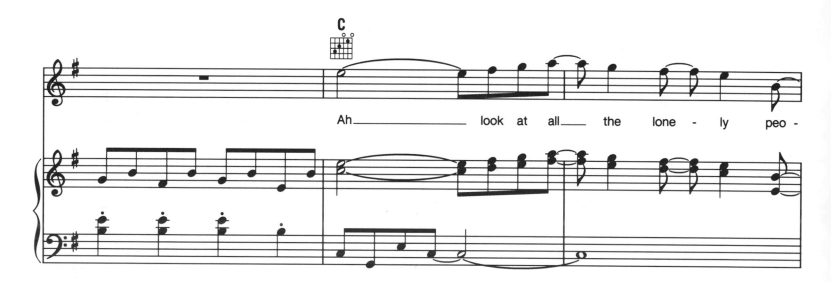

Ah_____ look at all___ the lone - ly peo -

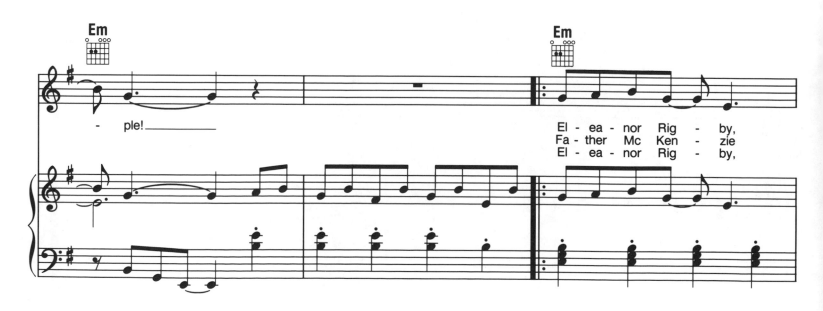

- ple!_____

El - ea - nor Rig - by,
Fa - ther Mc Ken - zie
El - ea - nor Rig - by,

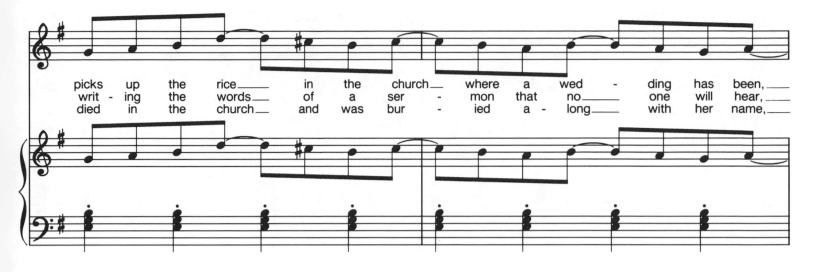

picks up the rice___ in the church___ where a wed - ding has been,___
writ - ing the words___ of a ser - mon that no___ one will hear,___
died in the church___ and was bur - ied a - long___ with her name,___

C

Em

___ lives in a dream.___ Waits at the win - dow,
___ no one comes near.___ Look at him work - ing,
___ no - bod - y came.___ Fa - ther Mc Ken - zie,

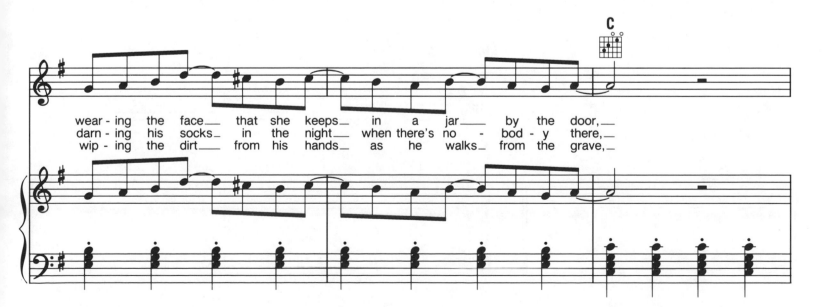

C

wear - ing the face___ that she keeps___ in a jar___ by the door,___
darn - ing his socks___ in the night when there's no - bod - y there,___
wip - ing the dirt___ from his hands___ as he walks___ from the grave,___

HARPER VALLEY P.T.A.

Words and Music by
TOM T. HALL

Moderately (with a heavy beat)

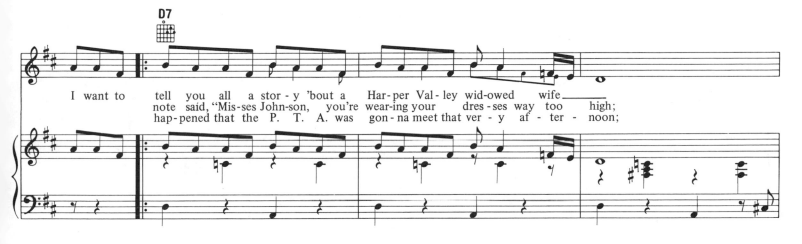

I want to tell you all a sto-ry 'bout a Har-per Val-ley wid-owed wife___
note said, "Mis-ses John-son, you're wear-ing your dres-ses way too high;
hap-pened that the P. T. A. was gon-na meet that ver-y af-ter-noon;

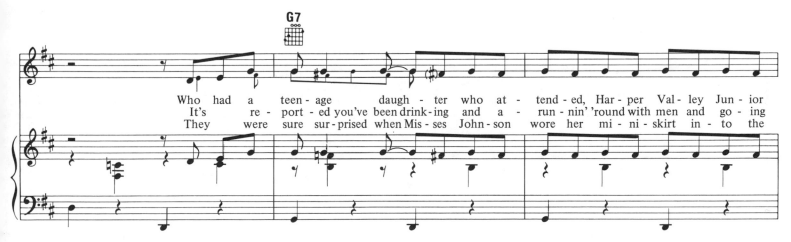

Who had a teen-age daugh-ter who at-tend-ed, Har-per Val-ley Jun-ior
It's re-port-ed you've been drink-ing and a-run-nin' 'round with men and go-ing
They were sure sur-prised when Mis-ses John-son wore her mi-ni-skirt in-to the

high.   Well   her daugh-ter came home__ one af-ter-
wild: And   we don't be-lieve you ought to be a-
room.   And as she walked up to the black-board,   I

noon, and did-n't ev - en stop to play;
bring-ing up your lit - tle girl this way."
still re-call the words she had to say;

She said, "Mom, I got a note here from the
It was signed by the sec - re - tar - y,
She said, "I'd like to ad - dress this meet-ing

Har-per Val-ley P. T. A."
Har-per Val-ley P. T. A."
of the Har-per Val-ley P. T. A."

The
Well, it
Well there's

Bob - by Tay-lor, sit - tin there, and sev - en times he's asked me for a date;
Har - per could-n't be here 'cause he stayed too long at Kel- ly's Bar a - gain,

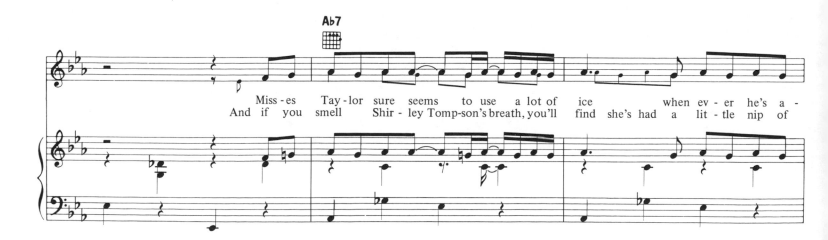

Miss - es Tay-lor sure seems to use a lot of ice when ev - er he's a -
And if you smell Shir - ley Tomp-son's breath, you'll find she's had a lit - tle nip of

way."
gin."

"And Mis - ter Bak - er, can you tell us why your
"Then you have the nerve to tell me you
would-n't put you on be - cause it

Ab7

sec - re-tar - y had to leave this town,
think that as a moth - er I'm not fit,
real - ly did, it hap-pened just this way,

And should-n't wid-ow Jones be told to keep her
Well, this is just a lit - tle Pey-ton Place, and
The day my Ma-ma socked it to the

Bb7   **Eb7**   To Coda   1   2   D.S. al Coda

win- dow shades all pulled com-plete-ly down?"
you're all Har - per Val - ley hyp - o crites."
Har - per Val - ley P. T. A.

Well Mis -ter

No, I

CODA   **Eb7**   **Ab7**   **Bb7**   **Eb7**

The day my Ma-ma socked it to the Har-per Val-ley P. T. A.

GENTLE ON MY MIND

Words and Music by
JOHN HARTFORD

83

2. It's not clinging to the rocks and ivy planted on their columns now that binds me
Or something that somebody said because they thought we fit together walkin'.
It's just knowing that the world will not be cursing or forgiving when I walk along
Some railroad track and find
That you're moving on the backroads by the rivers of my memory and for hours
You're just gentle on my mind.

3. Though the wheat fields and the clothes lines and junkyards and the highways
Come between us
And some other woman crying to her mother 'cause she turned and I was gone.
I still run in silence, tears of joy might stain my face and summer sun might
Burn me 'til I'm blind
But not to where I cannot see you walkin' on the backroads by the rivers flowing
Gentle on my mind.

4. I dip my cup of soup back from the gurglin' cracklin' caldron in some train yard
My beard a roughning coal pile and a dirty hat pulled low across my face.
Through cupped hands 'round a tin can I pretend I hold you to my breast and find
That you're waving from the backroads by the rivers of my memory ever smilin'
Ever gentle on my mind.

GIRL TALK
(From The Paramount Picture "HARLOW")

Words by BOBBY TROUP
Music by NEAL HEFTI

Slow and bluesy

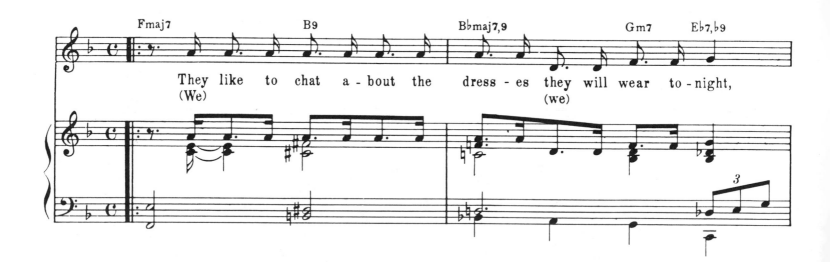

They like to chat a-bout the dress-es they will wear to-night,
(We)   (we)

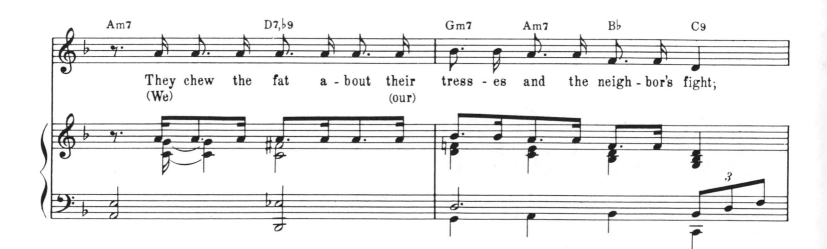

They chew the fat a-bout their tress-es and the neigh-bor's fight;
(We)   (our)

In - con - se - quen - tial things that men don't real - ly care to know

Be - come es - sen - tial things that wo - men find so "ap - pro - po".

But that's a dame, they're all the same; it's just a game. They call it
(we're)   (We)

GIRL   TALK,   GIRL   TALK.

They all me-ow a-bout the ups and downs of all their friends
(We)

The "who", the "how", the "why", they dish the dirt, it nev-er ends.
(we)

The weak-er sex, the speak-er sex we mor-tal males be-hold,
(you)

But tho' we joke we would-n't trade you for a ton of gold.

So ba - by stay and gab a way, but hear me say that af - ter
(It's all been planned, so take my hand, please un - der - stand the sweet - est

GIRL TALK, talk to
GIRL TALK talks of

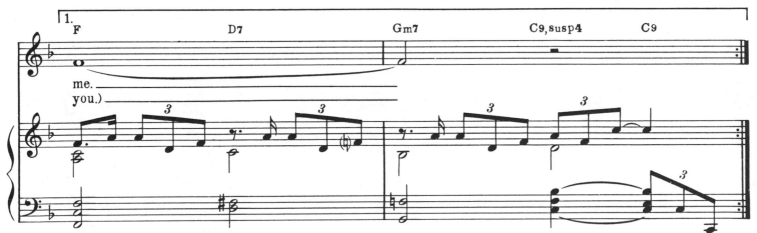

me.
you.)

me.
you.)

HE AIN'T HEAVY...HE'S MY BROTHER

Words and Music by BOB RUSSELL
and BOBBY SCOTT

Moderately slow, with feeling

mp

with pedal throughout

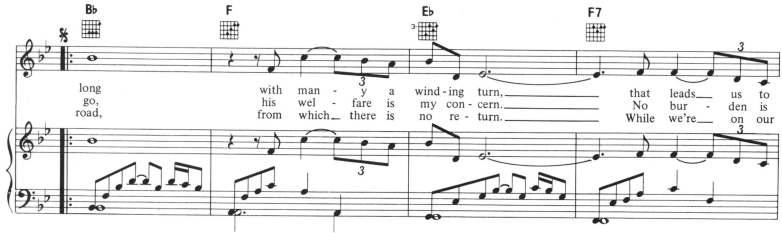

| Bb | F | Eb | F7 |

long
go, with man-y a wind-ing turn, that leads us to
road, his wel-fare is my con-cern. No bur-den is
from which there is no re-turn. While we're on our

| Gm | Ab | F11 |

who knows where, who knows where.
he to bear, we'll get there.
way to there, why not share?

But I'm
For I
And the

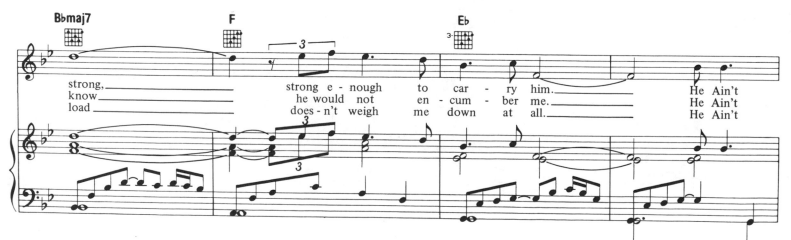

| Bbmaj7 | F | Eb |

strong, strong e-nough to car-ry him.
know he would not en-cum-ber me.
load does-n't weigh me down at all.

He Ain't
He Ain't
He Ain't

HERE COMES THE SUN

By GEORGE HARRISON

Here comes the sun, ___ doo da doo doo,

Here comes the sun, ___ and I say, "It's all ___ right."

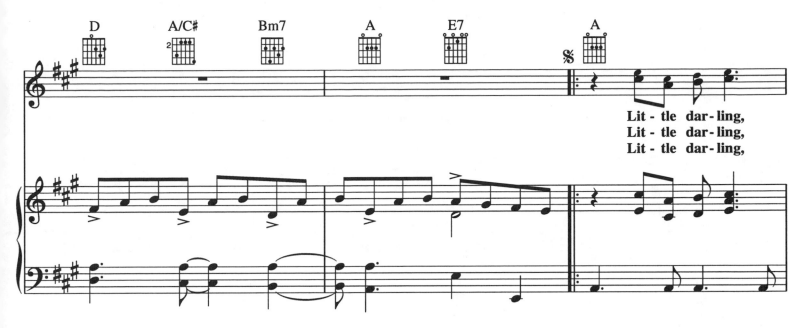

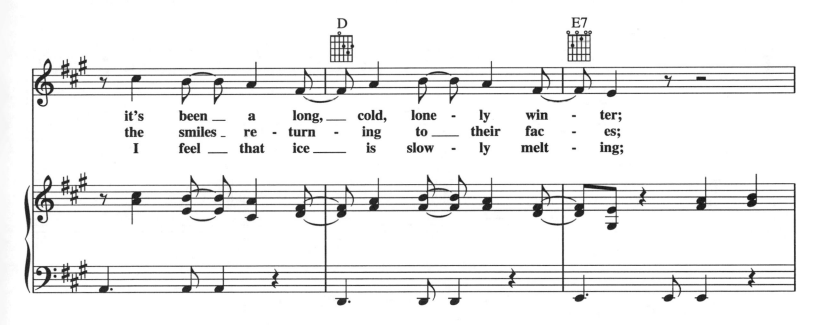

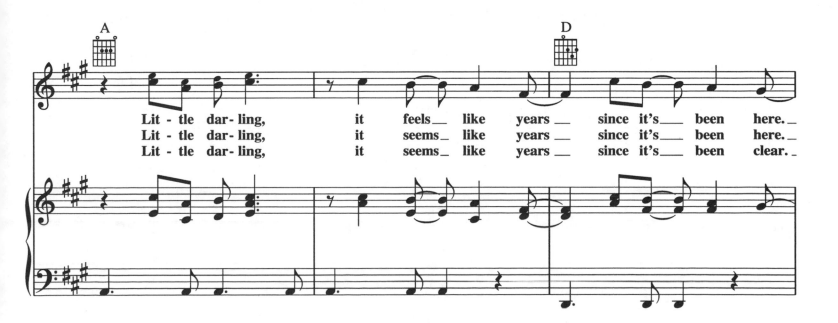

93

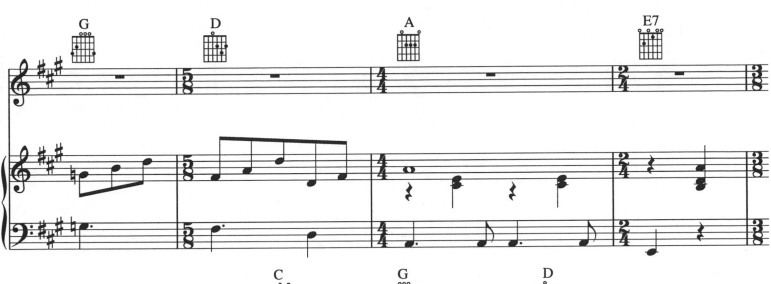

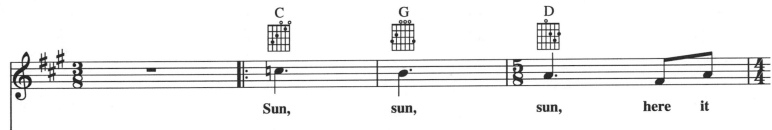

Sun,   sun,   sun,   here it

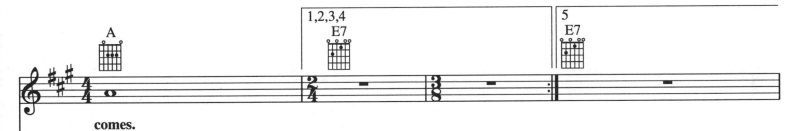

comes.

1,2,3,4
E7

5
E7

E7sus   E7   D.S. al Coda

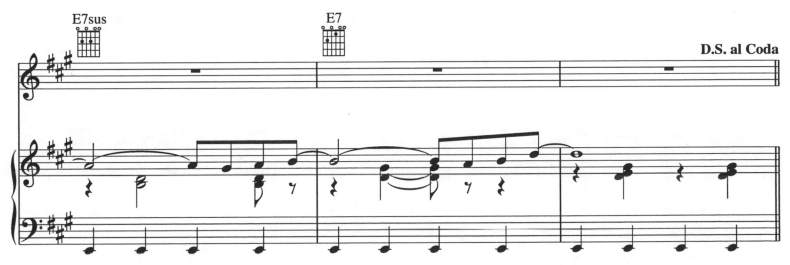

HOLLY HOLY

Words and Music by
NEIL DIAMOND

100

Hol - ly ho - ly dream, _

dream of on -

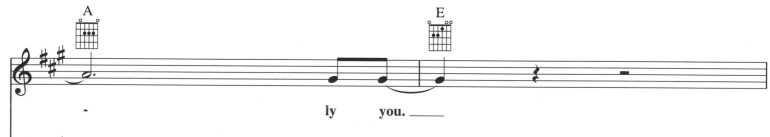

- ly you. _____

Hol - hol-ly ho - ho-ly sun. _

HURT SO BAD

Words and Music by TEDDY RANDAZZO,
BOBBY HART and BOBBY WEINSTEIN

103

I KNOW A PLACE

Words and Music by
TONY HATCH

MCA music publishing

I STARTED A JOKE

Words and Music by BARRY GIBB,
MAURICE GIBB and ROBIN GIBB

Moderately slow, in 2

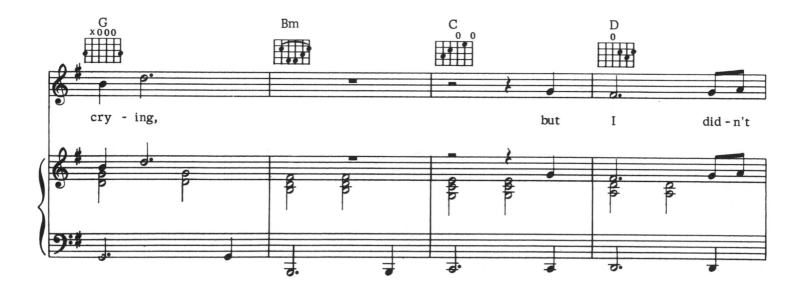

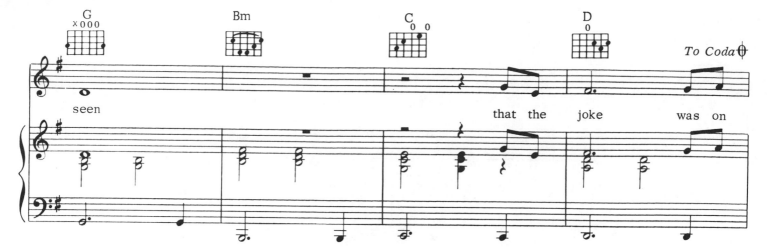

seen

that the joke was on

To Coda ⊕

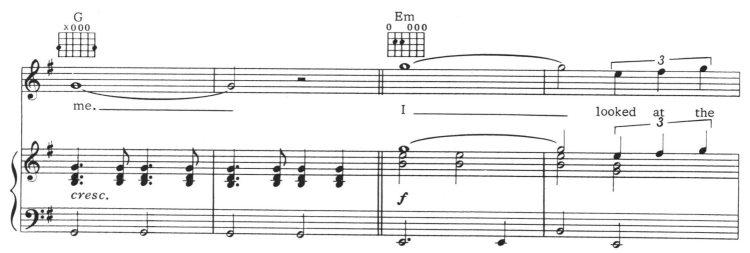

me._____ I_____ looked at the

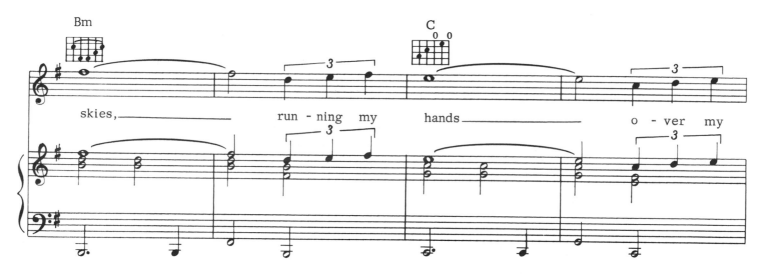

skies,_____ run - ning my hands_____ o - ver my

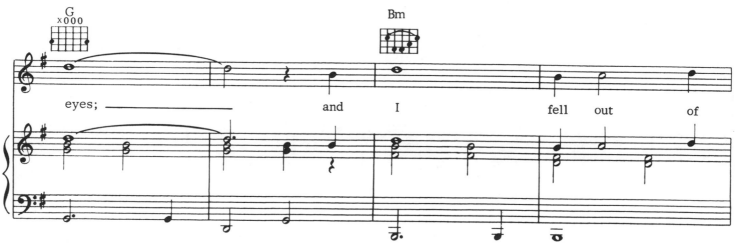

eyes;_____ and I fell out of

109

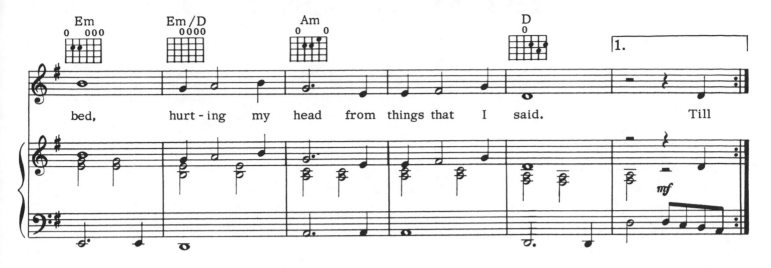

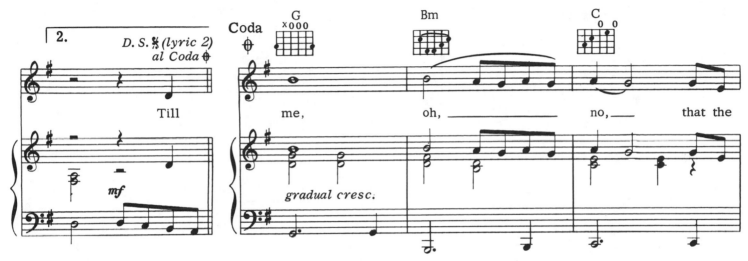

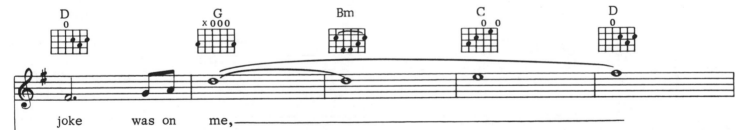

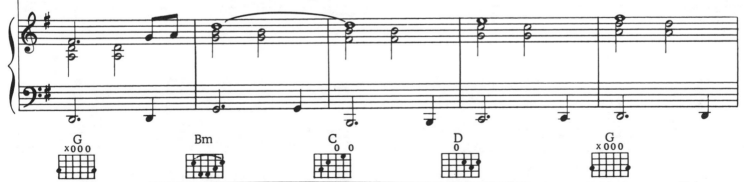

I WILL WAIT FOR YOU

Music by MICHEL LEGRAND
Original French Text by JACQUES DEMY
English Lyrics by NORMAN GIMBEL

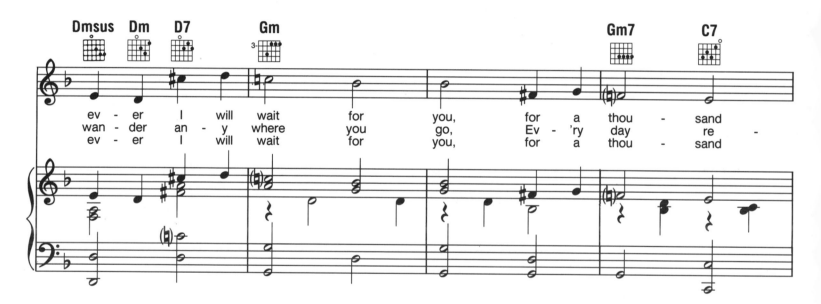

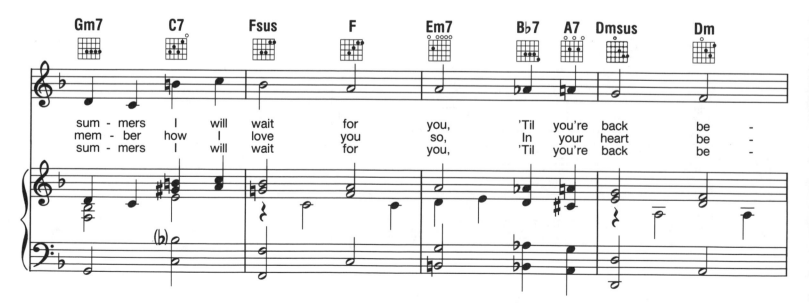

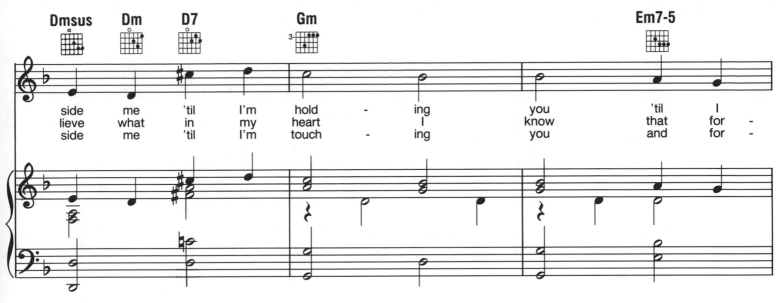

side me 'til I'm hold - ing you 'til I
lieve what in my heart I know that for -
side me 'til I'm touch - ing you and for -

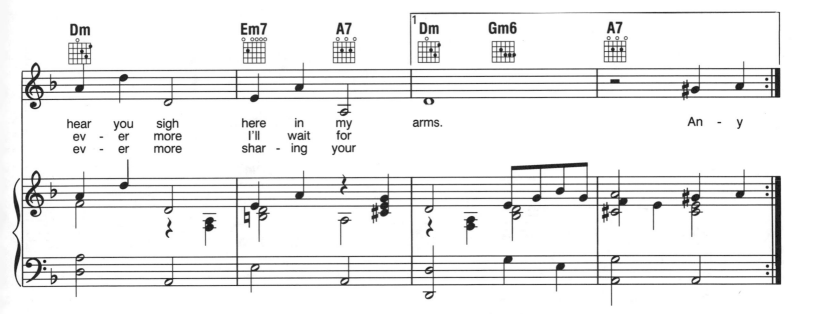

hear you sigh here in my arms. An - y
ev - er more I'll wait for
ev - er more shar - ing your

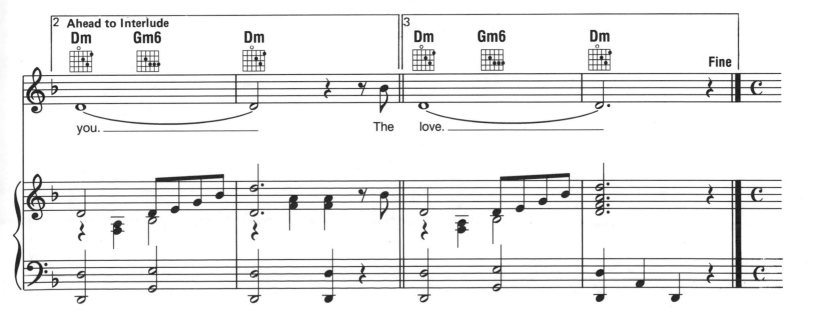

you. The love.

IF I RULED THE WORLD
(From "PICKWICK")

Words by LESLIE BRICUSSE
Music by CYRIL ORNADEL

Steady, moderate tempo

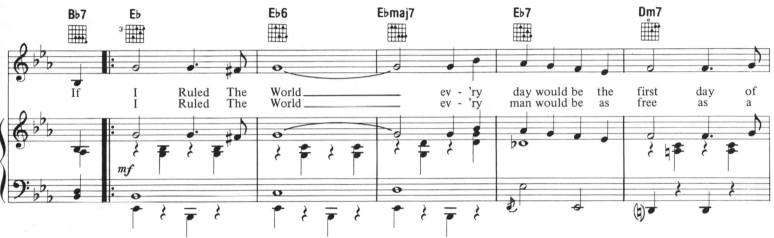

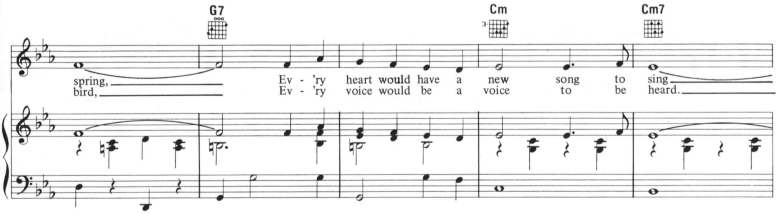

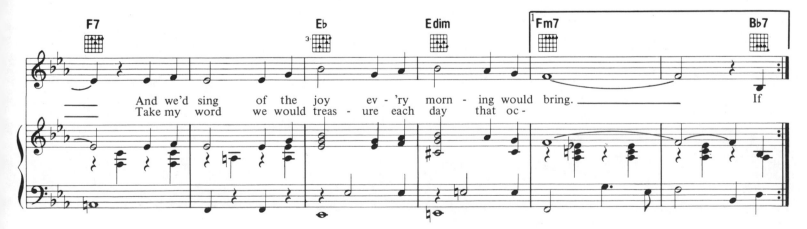

I'M SORRY

Words and Music by RONNIE SELF
and DUB ALBRITTEN

MCA music publishing

THE IMPOSSIBLE DREAM
(THE QUEST)
(From "MAN OF LA MANCHA")

Lyric by JOE DARION
Music by MITCH LEIGH

Tempo di Bolero

1. To dream the im-pos-si-ble dream, to
(2. To) right the un-right-a-ble wrong, to

fight the un-beat-a-ble foe, To
love pure and chaste from a-far, To

bear with un-bear-a-ble sor-row, to
try when your arms are too wea-ry, to

pause,_____ To be will-ing to march in-to hell for a heav-en-ly

cause! And I know,_____ if I'll on-ly be

true_____ To this glo-ri-ous quest,_____ that my

heart_____ will lie peace-ful and calm,_____ When I'm laid to my

IT'S NOW OR NEVER

Words and Music by AARON SCHROEDER
and WALLY GOLD

Moderately

Chorus

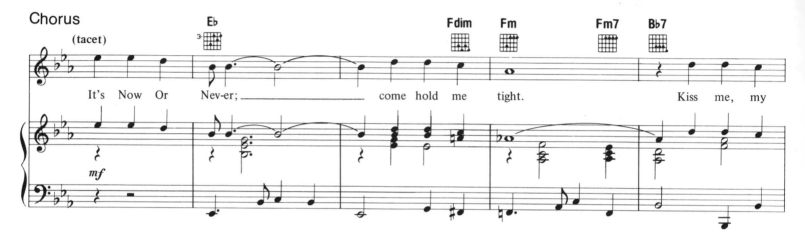

It's Now Or Nev-er; _____ come hold me tight. Kiss me, my

dar-lin'; _____ be mine to-night. _____ To-mor-row _____

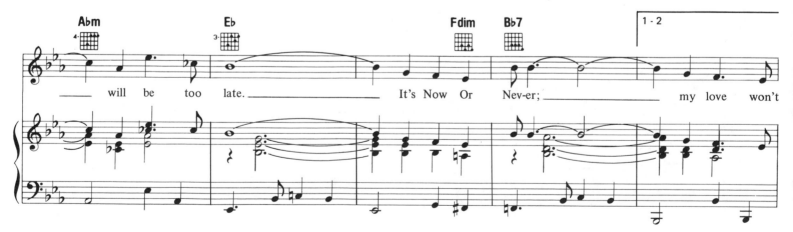

_____ will be too late. _____ It's Now Or Nev-er; _____ my love won't

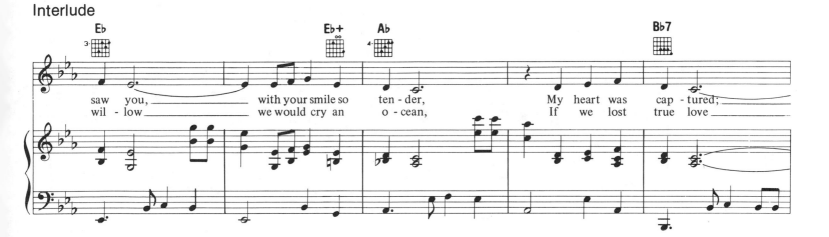

LEAVING ON A JET PLANE

Words and Music by
JOHN DENVER

'Cause I'm leav - in' on a jet plane, Don't know when

I'll be back a - gain. Oh babe, I hate to

go. _____ 2. There's so
3. _____

go. _____ 'Cause I'm

leav - in' on a jet plane, Don't know when I'll be back a - gain.

Repeat and Fade

MAGIC CARPET RIDE

Words and Music by RUSHTON MOREVE
and JOHN KAY

129

MARY IN THE MORNING

Words and Music by JOHNNY CYMBAL
and MIKE LENDELL

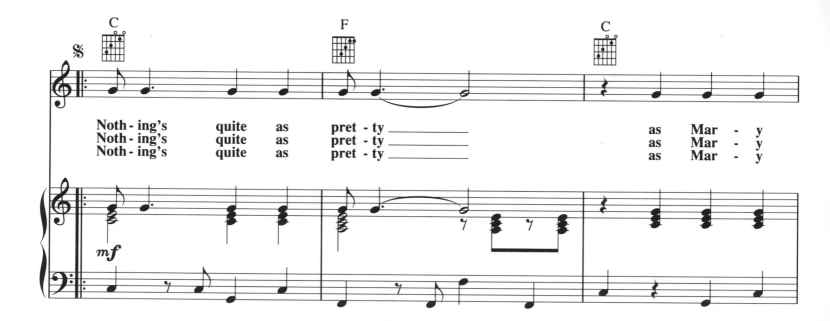

Noth-ing's quite as pret - ty _____ as Mar - y
Noth-ing's quite as pret - ty _____ as Mar - y
Noth-ing's quite as pret - ty _____ as Mar - y

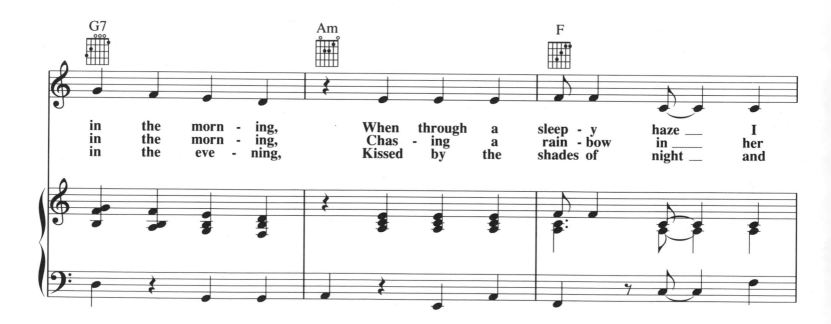

in the morn - ing, When through a sleep - y haze ___ I
in the morn - ing, Chas - ing a rain - bow in ___ her
in the eve - ning, Kissed by the shades of night ___ and

MCA music publishing

see her ly - ing there, / dreams so far a - way, / star - light in her hair, Soft as the / And when the she / And as we

rain to touch it / turns to touch it / walk, that falls on sum - mer flow - ers, / I kiss her face so soft - ly / I hold her close be - side me;

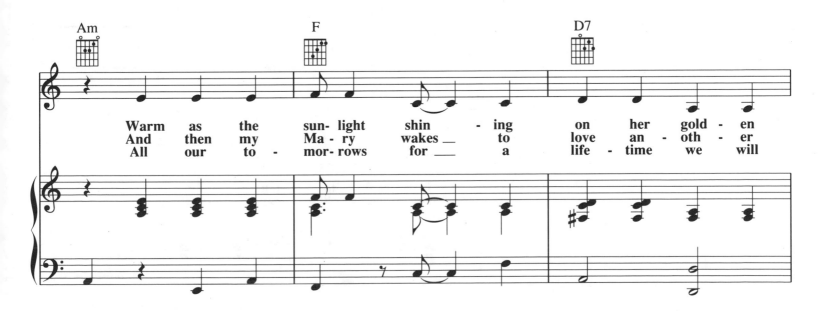

Warm as the sun - light shin - ing on her gold - en / And then my Ma - ry wakes to love an - oth - er / All our to - mor - rows for a life - time we will

MICHELLE

Words and Music by JOHN LENNON
and PAUL McCARTNEY

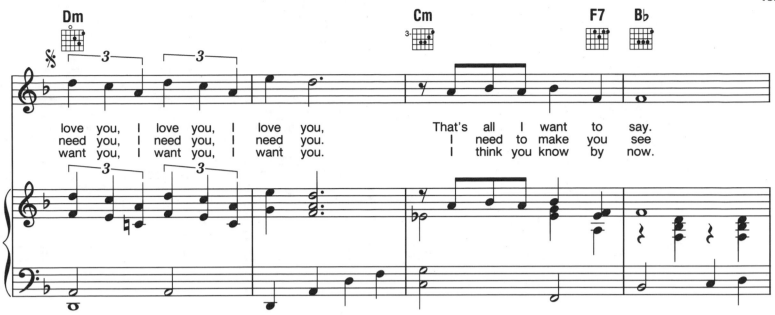

love you, I love you, I love you, That's all I want to say.
need you, I need you, I need you. I need to make you see
want you, I want you, I want you. I think you know by now.

Un - til I find a way _____ I will say the on - ly
what you mean to me. _____ Un - til I do, I'm
I'll get to you some - how. _____ Un - til I do, I'm

words I know that you'll un - der - stand.
hop - ing you will know what I mean. I
tell - ing you, so you'll un - der -

MR. ED

Words and Music by RAY EVANS
and JAY LIVINGSTON

MCA music publishing

MISSION: IMPOSSIBLE THEME

(From The Paramount Television Series "MISSION: IMPOSSIBLE")

By LALO SCHIFRIN

Moderately, with drive

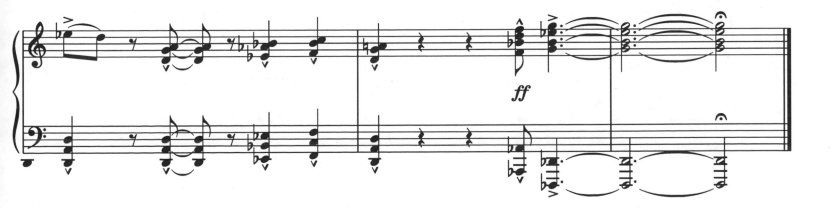

MOON RIVER
(From The Paramount Picture "BREAKFAST AT TIFFANY'S")

Words by JOHNNY MERCER
Music by HENRY MANCINI

MUSIC TO WATCH GIRLS BY

Driving rhythm

By SID RAMIN

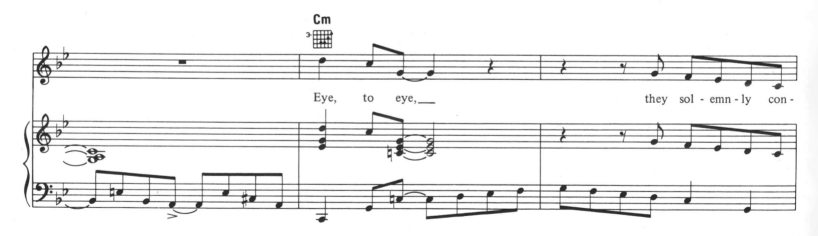

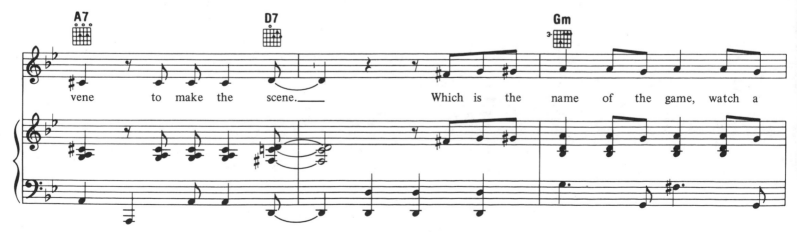

guy watch a dame on an-y street in town,_ up and down_

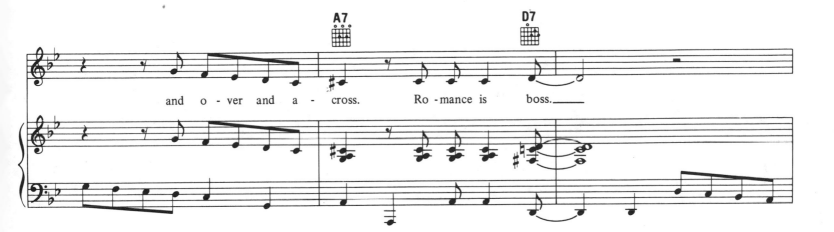

and o-ver and a-cross. Ro-mance is boss.____

Guys talk girl - talk, it hap-pens ev-'ry -

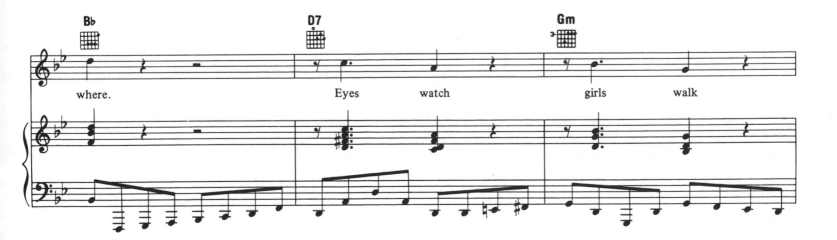

where. Eyes watch girls walk

146

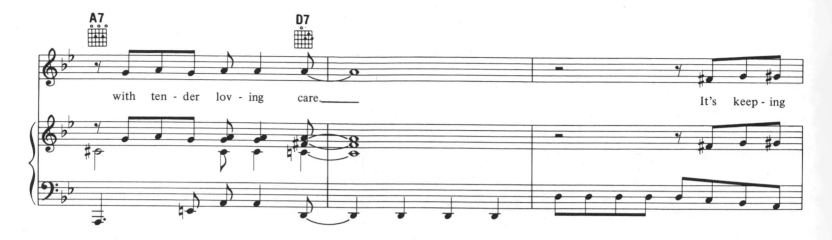

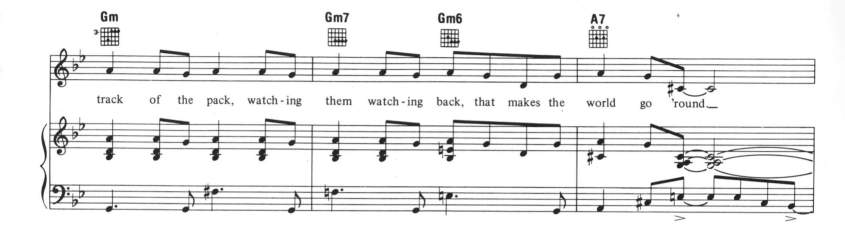

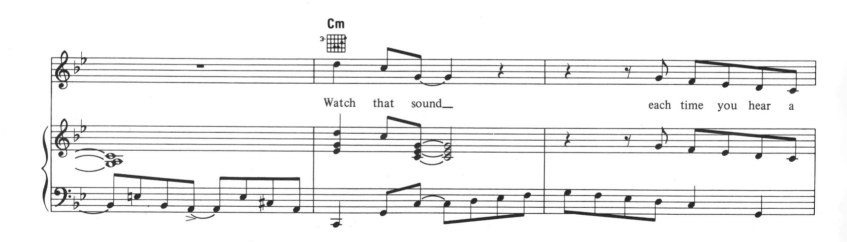

MY LOVE

Words and Music by
TONY HATCH

Moderato

Refrain

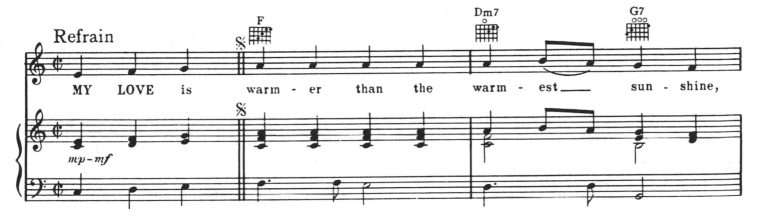

MY LOVE is warm-er than the warm-est___ sun-shine,

soft-er than a sigh,___ MY LOVE is deep-er than the

deep-est___ o-cean, wid-er than the sky._____ MY LOVE is

MCA music publishing

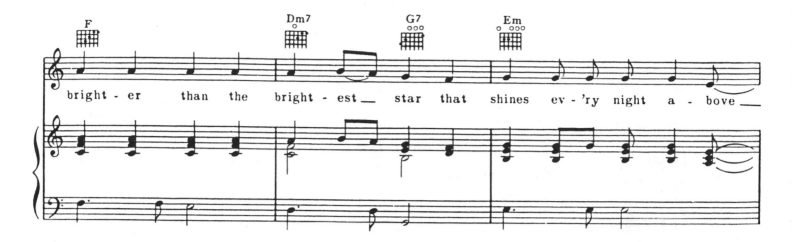

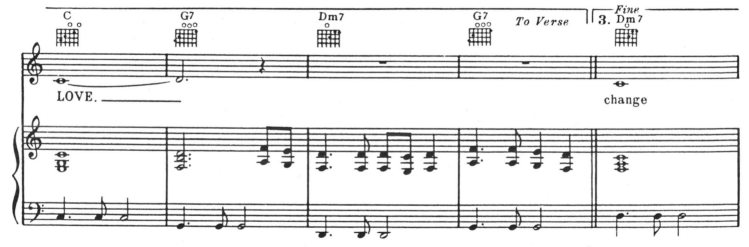

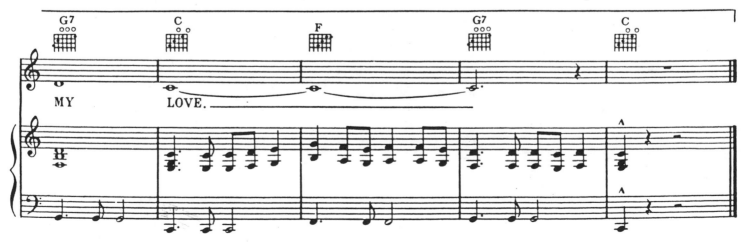

NEVER ON SUNDAY

(From Jules Dassin's Motion Picture "NEVER ON SUNDAY")

Words by BILLY TOWNE
Music by MANOS HADJIDAKIS

Moderato

Refrain

Oh, you can kiss me on a Mon - day, a Mon - day, a
cool day, a hot day, a

Mon - day is ver - y, ver - y good.
wet day, which - ev - er one you choose.

Or you can kiss me on a Tues - day, a Tues - day, a Tues - day, in fact I wish you
Or try to kiss me on a gray day, a May day, a pay day, and see if I re -

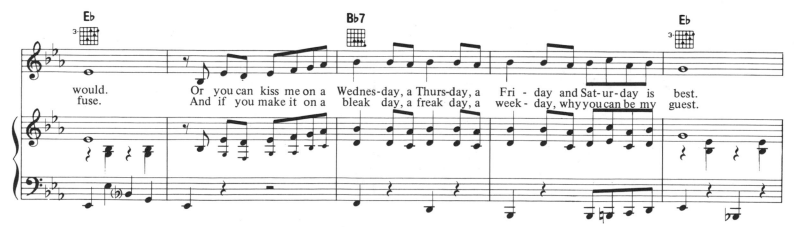

would.
fuse.

Or you can kiss me on a Wednes - day, a Thurs - day, a Fri - day and Sat - ur - day is best.
And if you make it on a bleak day, a freak day, a week - day, why you can be my guest.

151

PENNY LANE

Words and Music by JOHN LENNON
and PAUL McCARTNEY

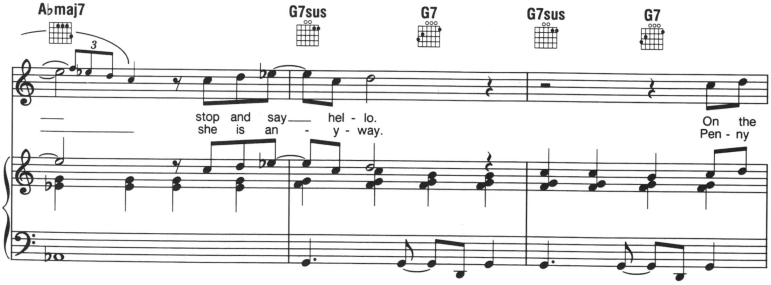

RETURN TO SENDER

Words and Music by OTIS BLACKWELL
and WINFIELD SCOTT

Moderate Rhythm and Blues

I gave a let-ter to the post-man; __ he put it in his
So then I dropped it in the mail-box __ and sent it Spe-cial

sack.
D.

Bright and ear-ly next morn-ing he
Bright and ear-ly next morn-ing it

brought my let-ter back. }
came right back to me. }

She wrote up-on it: Re-turn__ to send-er,

ad - dress un - known.   No such num - ber,

no such zone.   We had a quar - rel,

a lov - er's spat.   I write I'm sor - ry but my

let - ter keeps com - ing back.   zone.   This time I'm gon - na

RAINDROPS KEEP FALLIN' ON MY HEAD

Lyric by HAL DAVID
Music by BURT BACHARACH

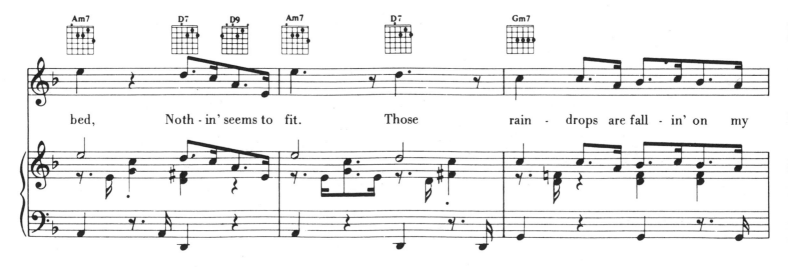

The blues__ they send__ to meet__ me won't de-feat__

__ me. It won't be long__ till hap-pi-ness__ steps up__

__ to greet me.__

Rain-drops keep fall-in' on my head, but that does-n't mean my eyes will

soon be turn - in' red. Cry - in's not for me 'cause

I'm nev - er gon - na stop the rain by com-plain-in'. Be - cause I'm

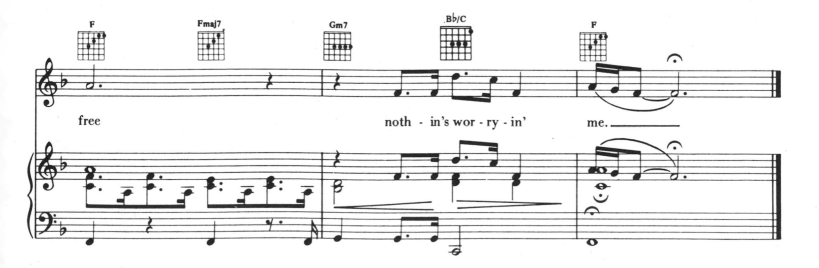

free noth - in's wor - ry - in' me.

RUBY, DON'T TAKE YOUR LOVE TO TOWN

Words and Music by
MEL TILLIS

Moderately

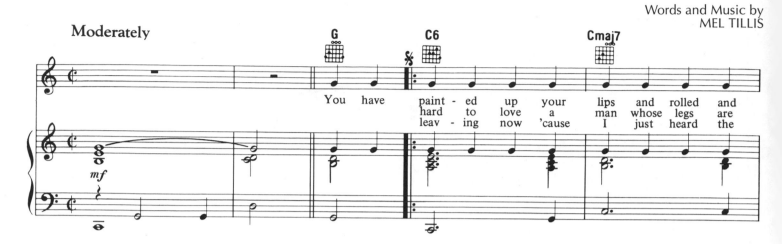

You have paint- ed up your lips and rolled and
hard to love a man whose legs are
leav - ing now 'cause I just heard the

curled your tint- ed hair.
bent and par - a - lized,
slam - ming of a door

Ru - by are you con - tem - plat - ing
And the wants and needs of a wo - man your age.
The way I know I've heard it slam one

go - ing out some - where?
Ru - by I re - a - lize,
hun - dred times be - fore,

The sha - dows on the wall tell me the
But it won't be long I've heard them say un -
And if I could move I'd get my gun and

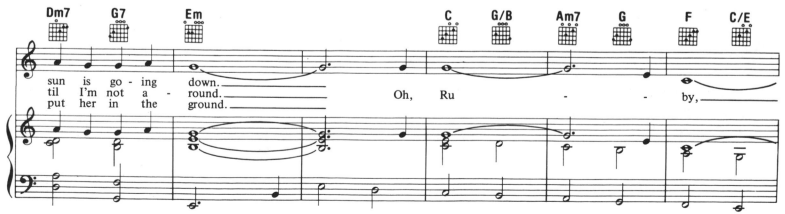

sun is go - ing down.
til I'm not a - round.
put her in the ground.

Oh, Ru - by,

RUNAWAY

Moderately bright

Words and Music by DEL SHANNON
and MAX CROOK

168

SEASONS IN THE SUN
(LE MORIBOND)

English Lyric by ROD McKUEN
Music by JACQUES BREL

Folk ballad style (Moderato)

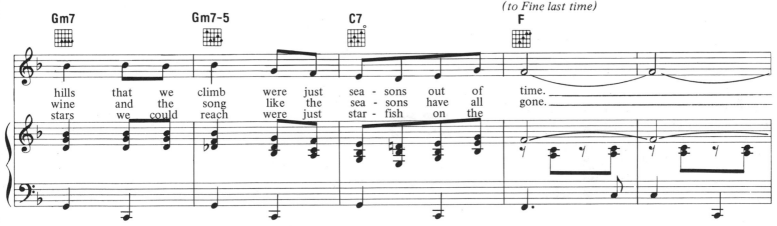

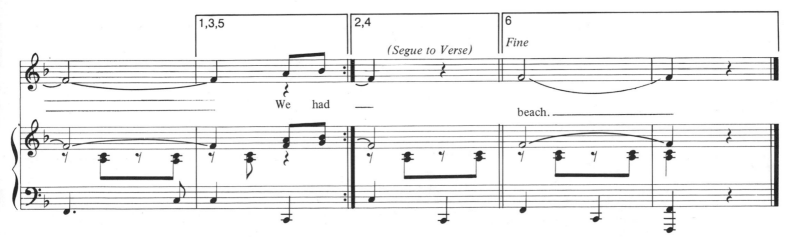

Verse

1. Good - bye to you, my trust - ed friend, _____
2. Good - bye, Pa - pa, please pray _____ for me, _____
3. Good - bye, Mich - elle, my lit - tle one, _____

We've known each oth - er since we were nine _____ or ten;
I was the black sheep of _____ the fam - i - ly;
You gave me love and helped _____ me find the sun;

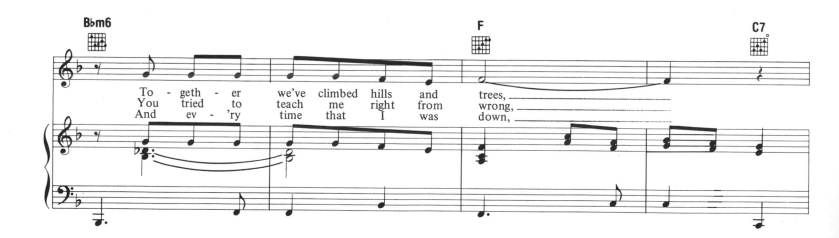

To - geth - er we've climbed hills and trees, _____
You tried to teach me right from wrong, _____
And ev - 'ry time that I was down, _____

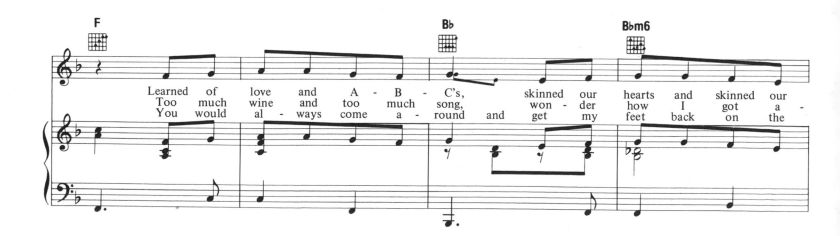

Learned of love and A - B - C's, skinned our hearts and skinned our
Too much wine and too much song, won - der how I
You would al - ways come a - round and get my feet back on the

171

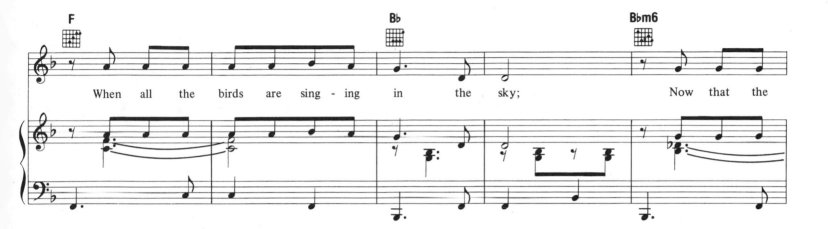

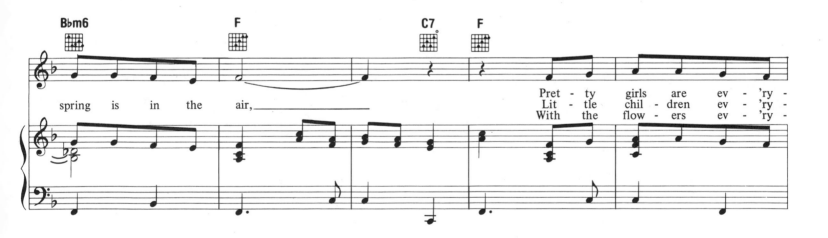

Save the Last Dance for Me

Words and Music by DOC POMUS
and MORT SHUMAN

much.   You can

dance,   go and car - ry on ___ till the night is gone ___ till it's

time   to   go. ___   If {he/she} asks   if you're

all   a - lone, ___   can {he/she} take   you home, ___ you've got to

SECRET AGENT MAN

Words and Music by P.F. SLOAN
and STEVE BARRI

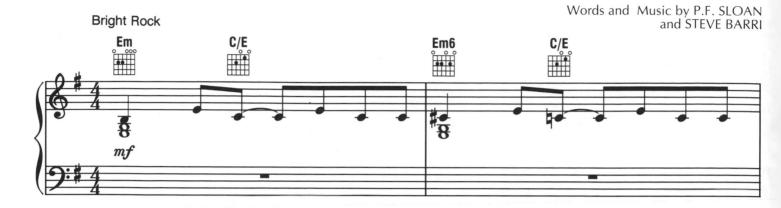

MCA music publishing

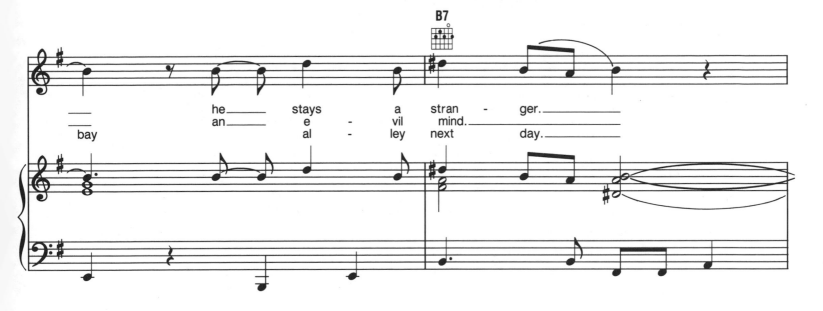

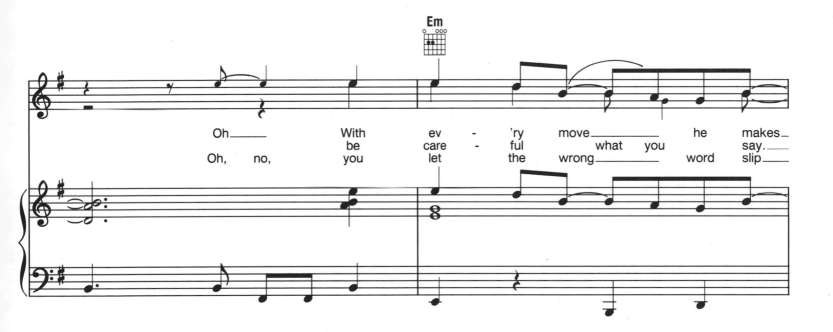

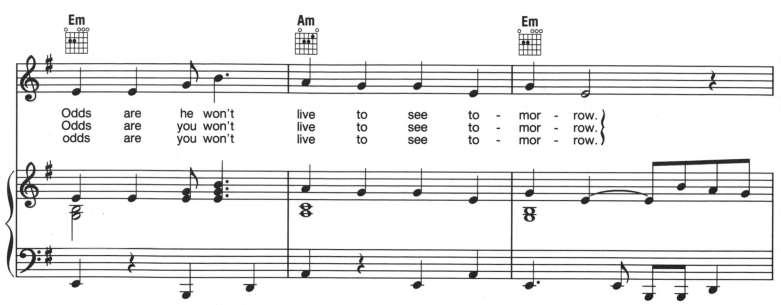

Odds are he won't live to see to - mor - row.
Odds are you won't live to see to - mor - row.
odds are you won't live to see to - mor - row.

Se - cret a - gent man,___ se - cret

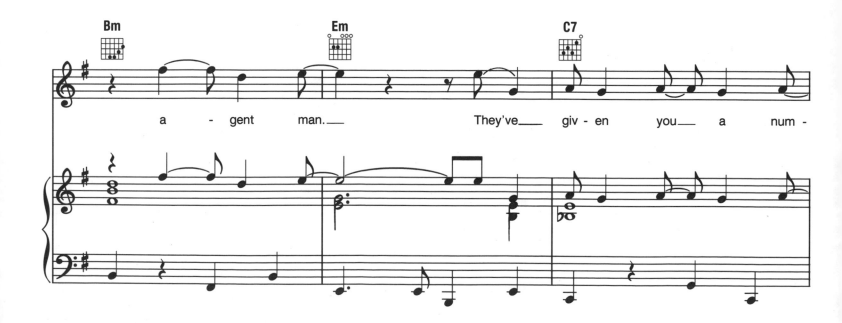

a - gent man.___ They've___ giv - en you___ a num-

SWEET CAROLINE

Words and Music by
NEIL DIAMOND

E

know it's grow - in' strong.

A   D

Was in the spring,_   and spring be -

A

came the sum - mer.   Who'd have be - lieved_ you'd come a -

E7   A

long?   Hands,
                Warm,

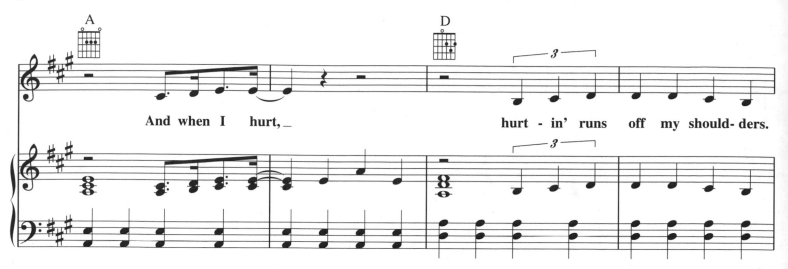

And when I hurt, __ hurt - in' runs off my should- ders.

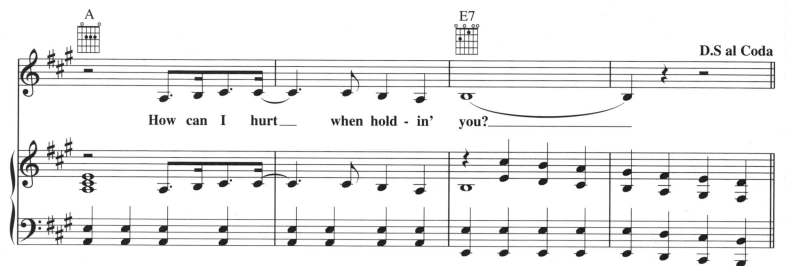

How can I hurt__ when hold - in' you?____

CODA

no chord

SUMMER SAMBA
(So Nice)

Original Words and Music by MARCOS VALLE
and PAULO SERGIO VALLE

Relaxed Bossa Nova

MCA music publishing

188

TELL LAURA I LOVE HER

Words and Music by JEFF BARRY
and BEN RALEIGH

192

193

TELL IT LIKE IT IS

Words and Music by GEORGE DAVIS
and LEE DIAMOND

A TIME FOR US
(LOVE THEME)
(From The Paramount Picture "ROMEO AND JULIET")

Words by LARRY KUSIK and EDDIE SNYDER
Music by NINO ROTA

TRUE GRIT
(Theme From The Paramount Picture "TRUE GRIT")

Words by DON BLACK
Music by ELMER BERNSTEIN

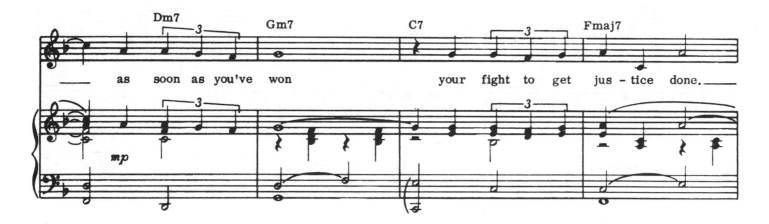

200

One day you will rise and you won't be-lieve your eyes.

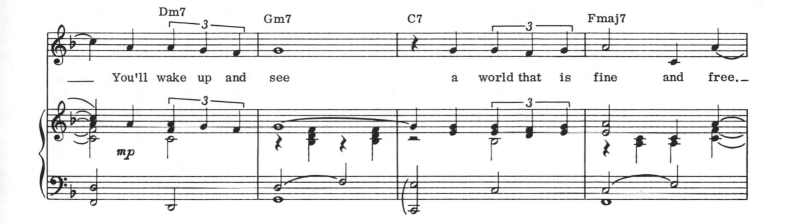

You'll wake up and see a world that is fine and free.

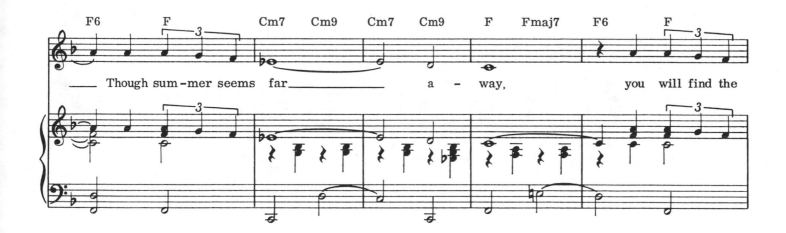

Though sum-mer seems far a-way, you will find the

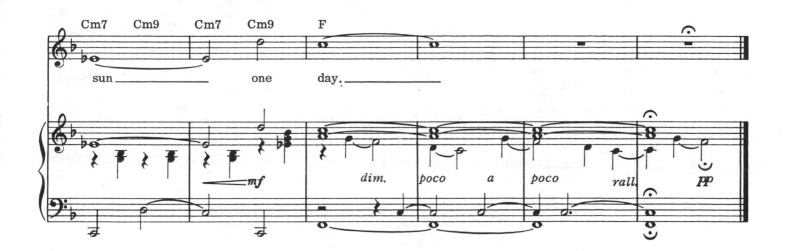

sun one day.

UNDER THE BOARDWALK

Words and Music by ARTIE RESNICK
and KENNY YOUNG

204

WOOLY BULLY

Words and Music by
DOMINGO SAMUDIO

1. Mat - ty told Hat - ty
2,3. *See additional lyrics*

A - bout a thing she saw.

Had two big horns

Bul - ly____

Additional Lyrics

2. Hatty told Matty
   Let's don't take no chance,
   Let's not be L 7
   Come and learn to dance
   Wooly bully — wooly bully —
   Wooly bully — wooly bully — wooly bully.

3 Matty told Hatty
  That's the thing to do,
  Get yo' someone really
  To pull the wool with you —
  Wooly bully — wooly bully
  Wooly bully — wooly bully — wooly bully.

WHAT THE WORLD NEEDS NOW IS LOVE

Lyric by HAL DAVID
Music by BURT BACHARACH

WHEN I'M SIXTY-FOUR

Words and Music by JOHN LENNON
and PAUL McCARTNEY

Moderately

When I get old - er, los - ing my hair___ man - y years from now___

___ Will you still be send - ing me a val - en - tine,___

MCA music publishing

215

WICHITA LINEMAN

Words and Music by
JIMMY WEBB

2

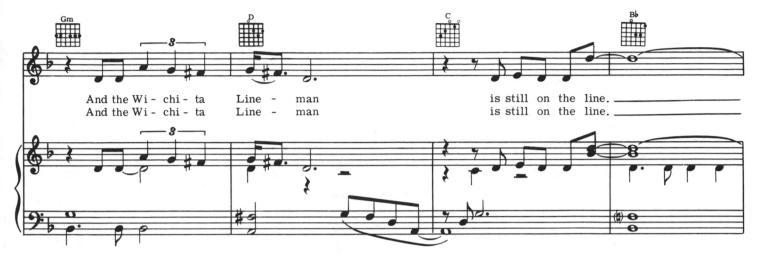

And the Wi - chi - ta   Line - man   is still on the line. _____

And the Wi - chi - ta   Line - man   is still on the line. _____

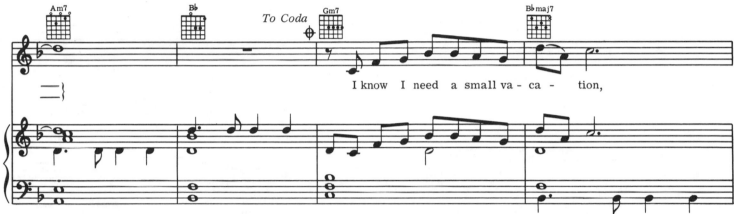

To Coda

I know I need a small va - ca - tion,

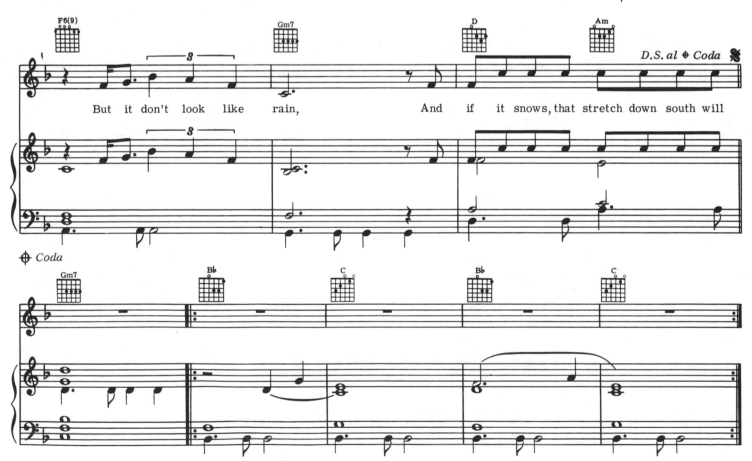

But it don't look like   rain,   And   if   it snows, that stretch down south will

D.S. al ⊕ Coda 𝄋

⊕ *Coda*

YELLOW SUBMARINE

Words and Music by JOHN LENNON
and PAUL McCARTNEY

221

Chorus:

THE DECADE SERIES

The Decade Series explores the music of the 1890's to the 1980's through each era's major events and personalities. Each volume features text and photos and over 40 of the decade's top songs, so readers can see how music has acted as a mirror or a catalyst for current events and trends. Each book is arranged for piano, voice & guitar.

Songs Of The 1890's

Over 50 songs, including: America, The Beautiful • The Band Played On • Hello! Ma Baby • Maple Leaf Rag • My Wild Irish Rose • O Sole Mio • The Sidewalks Of New York • The Stars And Stripes Forever • Ta Ra Ra Boom De Ay • Who Threw The Overalls In Mistress Murphy's Chowder • and more.

_____ 00311655 ....$12.95

Songs Of The 1900s – 1900-1909

Over 50 favorites, including: Anchors Aweigh • Bill Bailey, Won't You Please Come Home • By The Light Of The Silvery Moon • Fascination • Give My Regards To Broadway • Mary's A Grand Old Name • Meet Me In St. Louis • Shine On Harvest Moon • Sweet Adeline • Take Me Out to the Ball Game • Waltzing Matilda • The Yankee Doodle Boy • You're A Grand Old Flag • and more.

_____ 00311656 ....$12.95

Songs Of The 1910s

Over 50 classics, including: After You've Gone • Alexander's Ragtime Band • Danny Boy • (Back Home Again) In Indiana • Let Me Call You Sweetheart • My Melancholy Baby • 'Neath The Southern Moon • Oh, You Beautiful Doll • Rock-A-Bye Your Baby With A Dixie Melody • When Irish Eyes Are Smiling • You Made Me Love You • and more.

_____ 00311657 ....$12.95

Songs Of The 20's

58 songs, featuring: Ain't Misbehavin' • April Showers • Baby Face • California Here I Come • Five Foot Two, Eyes Of Blue • I Can't Give You Anything But Love • Manhattan • Stardust • The Varsity Drag • Who's Sorry Now.

_____ 00361122 ....$14.95

Songs Of The 30's

61 songs, featuring: All Of Me • The Continental • I Can't Get Started • I'm Getting Sentimental Over You • In The Mood • The Lady Is A Tramp • Love Letters In The Sand • My Funny Valentine • Smoke Gets In Your Eyes • What A Diff'rence A Day Made.

_____ 00361123 ....$14.95

Songs Of The 40's

61 songs, featuring: Come Rain Or Come Shine • God Bless The Child • How High The Moon • The Last Time I Saw Paris • Moonlight In Vermont • A Nightingale Sang In Berkeley Square • A String Of Pearls • Swinging On A Star • Tuxedo Junction • You'll Never Walk Alone.

_____ 00361124 ....$14.95

Songs Of The 50's

59 songs, featuring: Blue Suede Shoes • Blue Velvet • Here's That Rainy Day • Love Me Tender • Misty • Rock Around The Clock • Satin Doll • Tammy • Three Coins In The Fountain • Young At Heart.

_____ 00361125 ....$14.95

Songs Of The 60's

60 songs, featuring: By The Time I Get To Phoenix • California Dreamin' • Can't Help Falling In Love • Downtown • Green Green Grass Of Home • Happy Together • I Want To Hold Your Hand • Love Is Blue • More • Strangers In The Night.

_____ 00361126 ....$14.95

Songs Of The 70's

More than 45 songs including: Don't Cry For Me Argentina • Feelings • The First Time Ever I Saw Your Face • How Deep Is Your Love • Imagine • Let It Be • Me And Bobby McGee • Piano Man • Reunited • Send In The Clowns • Sometimes When We Touch • Tomorrow • You Don't Bring Me Flowers • You Needed Me.

_____ 00361127 ....$14.95

Songs Of The 80's

Over 40 of this decade's biggest hits, including: Candle In The Wind • Don't Worry, Be Happy • Ebony And Ivory • Endless Love • Every Breath You Take • Flashdance... What A Feeling • Islands In The Stream • Kokomo • Memory • Sailing • Somewhere Out There • We Built This City • What's Love Got To Do With It • With Or Without You.

_____ 00490275 ....$14.95

MORE SONGS OF THE DECADE SERIES

Due to popular demand, we are pleased to present these new collections with even more great songs from the 1920s through 1980s. Each book features piano/vocal/guitar arrangements. Perfect for practicing musicians, educators, collectors, and music hobbyists.

More Songs Of The '20s

Over 50 songs, including: Ain't We Got Fun? • All By Myself • Bill • Carolina In The Morning • Fascinating Rhythm • The Hawaiian Wedding Song • I Want To Be Bad • I'm Just Wild About Harry • Malaguena • Nobody Knows You When You're Down And Out • Someone To Watch Over Me • Yes, Sir, That's My Baby • and more.

_____ 00311647 ....$14.95

More Songs of the '30s

Over 50 songs, including: All The Things You Are • Begin The Beguine • A Fine Romance • I Only Have Eyes For You • In A Sentimental Mood • Just A Gigolo • Let's Call The Whole Thing Off • The Most Beautiful Girl In The World • Mad Dogs And Englishmen • Stompin' At The Savoy • Stormy Weather • Thanks For The Memory • The Very Thought Of You • and more.

_____ 00311648 ....$14.95

More Songs Of The '40s

Over 60 songs, including: Bali Ha'i • Be Careful, It's My Heart • A Dream Is A Wish Your Heart Makes • Five Guys Named Moe • Is You Is, Or Is You Ain't (Ma' Baby) • The Last Time I Saw Paris • Old Devil Moon • San Antonio Rose • Some Enchanted Evening • Steppin' Out With My Baby • Take The "A" Train • Too Darn Hot • Zip-A-Dee-Doo-Dah • and more.

_____ 00311649 ....$14.95

More Songs Of The '50s

Over 50 songs, including: All Of You • Blueberry Hill • Chanson D'Amour • Charlie Brown • Do-Re-Mi • Hey, Good Lookin' • Hound Dog • I Could Have Danced All Night • Love And Marriage • Mack The Knife • Mona Lisa • My Favorite Things • Sixteen Tons • (Let Me Be Your) Teddy Bear • That's Amore • Yakety Yak • and more.

_____ 00311650 ....$14.95

More Songs Of The '60s

Over 60 songs, including: Alfie • Baby Elephant Walk • Bonanza • Born To Be Wild • Eleanor Rigby • The Impossible Dream • Leaving On A Jet Plane • Moon River • Raindrops Keep Fallin' On My Head • Ruby, Don't Take Your Love To Town • Seasons In The Sun • Sweet Caroline • Tell Laura I Love Her • A Time For Us • What The World Needs Now • Wooly Bully • and more.

_____ 00311651 ....$14.95

More Songs Of The '70s

Over 50 songs, including: Afternoon Delight • All By Myself • American Pie • Billy, Don't Be A Hero • The Candy Man • Happy Days • I Shot The Sheriff • Long Cool Woman (In A Black Dress) • Maggie May • On Broadway • She Believes In Me • She's Always A Woman • Spiders And Snakes • Star Wars • Taxi • You've Got A Friend • and more.

_____ 00311652 ....$14.95

More Songs Of The '80s

Over 50 songs, including: Addicted To Love • Almost Paradise • Axel F • Call Me • Don't Know Much • Even The Nights Are Better • Footloose • Funkytown • Girls Just Want To Have Fun • The Heat Is On • Karma Chameleon • Longer • Straight Up • Take My Breath Away • Tell Her About It • We're In This Love Together • and more.

_____ 00311653 ....$14.95

FOR MORE INFORMATION, SEE YOUR LOCAL MUSIC DEALER,
OR WRITE TO:

HAL•LEONARD

7777 W. BLUEMOUND RD. P.O. BOX 13819 MILWAUKEE, WI 53213

Prices, availability & contents subject to change without notice.